"The Dark Side of Halloween & The Bewitching of America"

by David L. Brown, Th.M, Ph.D.

(c) September 1998 by David L. Brown
Re-issue September, 2018

ISBN: 978-1-7321746-3-4

Copies of this book are available by contacting:
Logos Communication Consortium, Inc.
P.O. BOX 173
Oak Creek, WI 53154
Phone: (414) 768-9754 Fax: (414) 762-8922
E-mail: PastorDavidLBrown@gmail.com

All Scripture quotes are from the King James Bible

WARNING

This book is **NOT** intended for children! It is written to warn parents and adults of abominations and perversions of Halloween, witchcraft and the occult.

ADDRESS ALL INQUIRES TO:
THE OLD PATHS PUBLICATIONS, INC.
142 GOLD FLUME WAY
CLEVELAND, GA 30528
TOP@theoldpathspublications.com
www.theoldpathspublications.com

Links to Amazon US, UK, CAD, and Barnes and Noble are located on the publisher's website.

TABLE OF CONTENTS

TABLE OF CONTENTS 3
INTRODUCTION 7
  Purpose 8
  My Past Association With Halloween 10
  Challenge, Research and Change 12
PART 1 15
  THE HISTORY OF HALLOWEEN 15
  More Information Confirming the Pagan, Idolatrous Origin of Halloween 17
  Ralph Linton wrote: 17
  Stonehenge 22
  The Nimrod - Druid Connection 23
  What Witches, Satanists and Other Occultists Say About Halloween 25
  Witch - Doreen Valiente: 25
  Witch - Margot Adler: 26
  Satanist - Anton Szandor LaVey (now deceased): 27
  Gothic & Vampire Cults: 27
  The Day of The Dead: 27
  Voodoo: 27
  Followers of Crowley: 28
  Halloween Is A Recognized Occult Holiday 28
  The Military Recognizes Halloween 29
  The Prison System Recognizes Halloween 29
  Halloween Specifics 32
  Where did the name Halloween come from? 32
  What is the origin of costumes? 34
  What is the origin of the bonfire? 35
  What is the origin of Trick or Treat? 36
  What is the origin and significance of the Jack-O-Lantern? 38
  What is the relationship black cats & cats in general have with Halloween? 41
  What is the significance of bobbing for apples? 43
  SUMMARY OF HALLOWEEN'S HISTORY 43
  THE HEROES OF HALLOWEEN 44
  The Witch 44
  The Origin of The Name "Witch" 47

The Dark Side of Halloween

The Influence of "the wickedest man in the world" on Wicca 47
Unmasking The Truth About Witches 50
LIES WITCHES TELL 54
Lie #1 - Witches Do Not Believe In or Acknowledge The Devil/Satan 54
Lie #2 - The upside-down pentagram is Satanic not Wiccan 56
Lie #3 - Witches only do good Magic, Healing Magic 56
Lie #4 - Witches don't believe in blood rituals, animal or human sacrifice 57
Definitions, Doctrines & Principles 60
WHAT DO WITCHES BELIEVE? 61
COMMON WITCHCRAFT & OCCULT BELIEFS 62
THE QUEST FOR WISDOM & POWER 69
The Means That God Approves For Accessing His Wisdom & Power 70
How People Attempt To Access Demonic Wisdom 71
FOUR CATEGORIES OF SUPERNATURAL PHENOMENA ... 76
THE HEROES OF HALLOWEEN 79
Vampires, Werewolves 79
The History of Vampires & Werewolves 79
What about werewolves? 80
A Look At Dracula 83
THE HARM OF HALLOWEEN 87
Let's review. Halloween is harmful because 98
Where The Occult Will Lead Its Followers 99
Christ Honoring Alternatives 106
PART 2 109
THE BEWITCHING OF AMERICA 109
THE PROBLEM WITH MYTHS 117
The Bible & Mythology 118
What does the Bible say about mythology? 119
What should be our response to myths? 123
Cartoons & Animated Movies 124
Bewitched By Dungeons & Dragons 127
THE ELEMENTS OF FANTASY ROLE PLAYING GAMES ... 128
MYTHOLOGY & IDOL WORSHIP 129
Magic Cards 139
The Yardstick for Determining Acceptability 144

TABLE OF CONTENTS

BIBLICAL GUIDELINES FOR DETERMINING ACCEPTABILITY.. 147
   What belief system is being promoted?.................... 147
   What philosophy or system of values does the game promote?.. 147
   Is there a "power" portrayed and if so, what is the source or origin of it? 151
   Where are the person's imagination and thoughts being directed? 152
   Does it magnify fear, glorify evil, promote violence, gore or death?.. 154
   FEAR 154
   EVIL & VIOLENCE... 155
   Are occult, New Age or other pagan practices included? 156
   Is it sensual or vulgar?'... 157
   DON'T PLAY RUSSIAN ROULETTE WITH YOUR SOUL!.. 158
   What does it mean to play Russian Roulette with your soul? 160
   Seven Common Ways People Play Russian Roulette With Their Souls.. 161
ENDNOTES—PART 1.. 173
ENDNOTES—PART 2.. 176
ABOUT THE AUTHOR... 179

The Dark Side of Halloween

INTRODUCTION

> **And have no fellowship with the unfruitful works of darkness, but rather reprove them.** Ephesians 5:11
>
> **Whatsoever ye do, do all to the glory of God.**
> 1 Corinthians 10:31

The sidewalks are swarming with excited children and young people masquerading as every imaginable creature and character...witches, animals, vampires, ghosts, mummies, cartoon characters, alien beings, clowns, devils, skeletons, hideous looking monsters, bloody mutilated beings and more. These kids go door to door shouting, 'Trick or Treat," hoping to collect a "ton" of candy before the night is over.

Take a look at the houses and yards the children are approaching. Many of them are decorated in a bizarre motif. Tombstones, graves with body parts exposed, ghosts, caldrons, supposed bodies hung by the neck are scattered around the yard and in the trees. Eerie grinning Jack-O-Lanterns watch as the children approach. Skeletons, scarecrows, witches, black cats, etc. decorate the doors and windows.

Oh yes, then there is an array of seasonal entertainment. The "haunted house" is easy enough to spot. You'll be able to find it by the long line and the strange sounds coming out of the old mansion. Likely you will find a group of kids talking about what they've just seen inside...the bloody body in the bathtub, the axe wielding maniac that chased them, the monster that jumped out swinging at them with a chain saw, the body hanging by the neck in the closet, and the refrigerator in the kitchen filled with bloody body parts.

Then, across town there are parties going on, perhaps at school or at a friend's house. The activities are different than the usual party though. There is a group playing with the OUIJA board trying to get it to work and tell them about their futures. Some are watching the latest horror video. Others meet at the graveyard in an effort to contact the dead. Still others are initiated into witchcraft to become "real" witches. Then there are those who go out into the night to raise havoc.

By now you have guessed what is going on. It's HALLOWEEN. To most people it seems like harmless fun. BUT, beneath Halloween's candy coating is a history of diabolical evil, evil that is directly connected to the occult, witchcraft and satanism. You need to be warned of this evil!

Purpose

The purpose of this book is to make you aware of the dark side of Halloween and show you how the demonic principles and practices are beguiling our children and our culture. I have researched this topic for nearly two decades and there is absolutely

INTRODUCTION

no doubt about Halloween's occult connection. Halloween has been the occultists' most effective tool in **bewitching America!** It has been and is being used by occultists of all stripes to interject their demonic doctrines into our culture.

It was 1984 when I released the first printed edition of this book under the title, **Halloween: Behind The Mask.** It included only 16 pages of information exposing Halloween's occult connection. As a result of that little book, I had the opportunity to present the material in churches, at rallies, in Christian schools and on Christian radio and TV programs. Many people were skeptical at first. To my surprise, some of the most antagonistic people I encountered were pastors and heads of Christian ministries and colleges. Many insisted that I was over reacting and that Halloween was just harmless fun. I must tell you, by and large, that is not the response I am getting today. Indeed "the mask" is off of the unholy day. Witches are out of the "broom closet" and peddling their demonic wares on television, in the newspapers, in the bookstores, and in the public schools. Speaking of the public schools. What is happening in your school district? I get calls from around the nation telling me that the Christian celebrations of Christmas (the birth of Christ) and Easter (the resurrection of Christ) are snubbed, maligned and even expelled from some public schools, but, not the occult holiday of Halloween! That is the public school's biggest holiday. Children are often

The Dark Side of Halloween

required to write reports on witchcraft. There are public schools that have even brought in witches to tell about their "wonderful, wholesome" religion. In the public schools, witchcraft is "IN" and Christianity is "OUT." While many Christians are waking up to the dark side of Halloween, Americans in general are increasingly being exposed to occult principles and adopting occult practices. Americans are being bewitched. Now, before I jump too far ahead, let's look at The History, The Heroes and The Harm of Halloween.

My Past Association With Halloween

Are you still celebrating Halloween? If you are, I want you to know that I took part in Halloween activities until 1981. That is when I discovered the demonic occult roots of Halloween. Previously, I had been ignorant of the truth about Halloween. But, once I realized the truth about Halloween, the Holy Spirit convicted me that I must obey **Ephesians 5:11** *"Have NO fellowship with the unfruitful works of darkness, but rather reprove (expose) them."* Let me share with you some more of the specifics of my involvement with Halloween and how the Lord lead me to renounce the celebration of Halloween.

There are three holidays that nearly every American kid loves; Christmas, Easter and Halloween! I was no different than any other American kid. I looked forward to them all. But there was one holiday that had a dark side, a side

INTRODUCTION

that I didn't like, a side that made me very uneasy. That holiday was Halloween. To be sure I liked the candy and I have a "ton" of silver in my teeth to prove it. As I moved into my teen years, I outgrew trick-or-treating or rather, I was told I was too old. My focus became the Halloween parties and dances that were the "in thing" for teenagers. I remember serving on the committee for our Junior Class Halloween party. My job was decorations. So I went to a long forgotten, overgrown, pre-Civil War era cemetery and took a broken tombstone and used it as a part of my Halloween decorations. I felt uneasy about what I had done and to make matters worse, when I cleaned up the old tombstone, I discovered that the person had died on my birthday, January 20th.

That really made me uneasy. I looked at that as a bad omen. The party could not get over soon enough for me. I wanted to get that tombstone back to where I had found it, and I did! You might say, "You were too superstitious!" I would agree. But that is just a part of the aura of evil associated with what I call "the dark side of Halloween." Underneath that thin candy coating there was a core of evil and a focus on death and the occult which had always made me uneasy.

My association with Halloween did not stop after high school unfortunately. Even after I entered the

ministry and up until 1980 I had taken church youth groups on NIGHTMARE OUTINGS sponsored by an international Christian youth organization. I sponsored Halloween parties in the churches that I pastored. Halloween was the only day I associated with witches, witchcraft, the occult and the devil.

Challenge, Research and Change

Prove all things; hold fast that which is good. Abstain from all appearance of evil. 1 Thessalonians 5:21-22

What changed my mind about Halloween? It was an article in a 1975 issue of Moody Monthly Magazine. I was leafing through a back issue when an article by Joy A. Sterling caught my eye entitled, **We Should Unmask Halloween**. I had missed the article previously. I read the article carefully and reread it again. She wrote in part...

> We evangelicals cringe at the descriptions of Satan worship in books and shudder at occult rites. But we dress our children as witches and devils and send them out to trick or treat. ...Whenever the apostles met persons connected with fortune-telling, witchcraft or the occult, the Holy Spirit

INTRODUCTION

dealt firmly and swiftly with them. When revival came to Ephesus, the occult books were the first to go (Acts 19:18-19). Anything that conjures up the spirits of evil has to go. And I believe that the symbols of Halloween do conjure up the spirits of evil. Not deliberately, not openly perhaps. But the devil never has been noted for working openly. He tries to convince people that he doesn't exist. And what better way to deny his power and identity than to tell children and their parents that witches, ghosts, fortune-tellers and devils are 'just for fun?[1]

Her article really troubled me. I thought, if what this lady says is true, I need to rethink my involvement in Halloween activities. I decided to research Halloween on my own and see if there was anything to what she was saying. WOW! WAS I SHOCKED by what I discovered. What she wrote was indeed true! I indeed had to change my ways. I decided not to celebrate Halloween.

I need to add this note. Many years later *Moody Monthly* published another article on Halloween. I must tell you how saddened I was when I read *Getting a Handle On Halloween*, by Linda Shepherd in the October 1993 issue of *Moody Monthly* that justified participation in Halloween activities. She rationalized her participation in Halloween activities with these words –

The Dark Side of Halloween

> "I felt good. I had loved and been loved by my neighbors."[2]

Truth is never to be sacrificed on the altars of feeling and love. The Apostle John wrote in **1 John 2:15:**

> *Love not the world, neither the things that are in the world ....*

PART 1

THE HISTORY OF HALLOWEEN

> He caused his children to pass through the fire in the valley of the son of Hinnom: also he observed times, and used enchantments, and used witchcraft, and dealt with a familiar spirit, and with wizards: he wrought much evil in the sight of the LORD, to provoke him to anger. 2 Chronicles 33:6

Our Pilgrim forefathers knew well of Halloween's occult roots. In fact they banned celebrating Halloween in America. Halloween was not celebrated in this country until 1845. At that time multiplied thousands of Irish emigrants flooded into New York because of the Irish Potato Famine of 1845-46. They brought with them an old Druid Holiday they called Halloween. Gradually celebrating this day spread throughout the rest of the country.

To understand Halloween's roots better we need to go back further into history and take a look at the Druids and the Celtic people. The Druids were the pagan priests of the Celts. They were idolaters, occult practitioners and witches of sorts. Let's begin with the information found in the 11th edition of the Encyclopedia Britannica.

> Halloween and its former attendant ceremonies long antedate Christianity. The two chief characteristics of ancient Halloween were the lighting of bonfires

The Dark Side of Halloween

and the belief that of all nights in the year this is the one during which ghosts and witches are most likely to wander abroad. Now on or about the 1st of November the Druids held their great autumn festival and lighted fires in honor of the Sun-god in thanks-giving of the harvest. Further, it was a Druidic belief that on the eve of this festival Saman, lord of death, called together the wicked souls that within the past twelve months had been condemned to inhabit the bodies of animals. Thus it is clear that the main celebration of Halloween was purely Druidical, and this is further proved by the fact that in parts of Ireland the 31st of October was, and even still is, known as Oidhche Shamhna, "Vigil of Saman." On the Druidic ceremonies were grafted some of the character-istics of the Roman festival in honor of Pamona held about the 1st of November.

Depending on your source material, the Druid Lord of Death and evil spirits was called Saman, Shamhan, Samana, Shamhain or Samhain. I have received numerous letters and e-mail from witches telling me there was no such Druid god. Yet, in the source material that I have used, (see the above quote), such as the historic 11th edition of Encyclopedia Britannica, it identifies the Druid Lord of Death as **Saman** and his holiday named after him as **Oidhche Shamhna**, translated "Vigil of Saman."

PART 1

Other reliable sources call his "holiday" The Vigil Samhain" (Shamhain is pronounced so-wein). I ask you, are the protests of the occult community an effort to "white wash" the truth about Saman and how they worshipped him in fiendish, bloody worship rituals? I believe that is probable.

Suffice it to say, at this point that the pagan worship day Samhain evolved into Halloween. But what of their Lord of Death? You probably have seen a modern day version of SAMAN without even knowing it. This pagan god was shown as a ghostly, skeleton holding a sickle in his hand. He later came to be known as THE GRIM REAPER.

More Information Confirming the Pagan, Idolatrous Origin of Halloween

> **Thou shalt not do so unto the LORD thy God: for every abomination to the LORD, which he hateth, have they done unto their gods; for even their sons and their daughters they have burnt in the fire to their gods.**
> Deuteronomy 12:31

Ralph Linton wrote:

The American celebration (of Halloween) rests upon Scottish and

The Dark Side of Halloween

> Irish folk customs which can be traced in a direct line from pre-Christian times. The earliest celebrations were held by the DRUIDS in honor of Shamhain, Lord of Death, whose festival fell on November 1st. [4]

Another source adds this information. November 1st was the Celtic New Year. That day was considered the day of death because temperatures were dropping, the tree leaves were falling, and it was getting dark sooner and staying dark longer. They believed their sun god, identified in the World Book Encyclopedia as Muck Olla[5], was losing strength because Saman, Lord of Death, was overpowering him. Remember, it was a Druidic belief that on the eve of the Vigil of Saman, October 31, the Lord of Death called together the wicked souls that within the past twelve months had been condemned to inhabit the bodies of animals as punishment for their evil deeds. This demon god then allowed them to return to their former homes to visit the living. Supposedly, to appease the Lord of Death and keep the spirits from harming the people, Druid priests led the people in diabolical worship ceremonies in which horses, cats, black sheep, oxen, human beings and other offerings were rounded up, stuffed into wicker cages and burned to death. Again, I have received correspondence from witches that dispute my asser-tion that Druids offered human sacrifices. Once again, I will reaffirm my position that they did offer human sacrifices, based on my research.

PART 1

Allow me to provide the evidence.

In his definitive book, *The Druids*, by Stuart Piggott you can read the following:

> Our information on Druid ceremonies mainly centers on sacrifice, and is contained in the Posidonian sources and in Pliny. Strabo writes ...of human sacrifice by shooting to death by arrows, or by impaling, and the holocaust of human and animal victims alike in a huge wicker figure (kolosson). Caesar likewise describes these great figures (immani magnitudine simulacra) whose limbs were filled with living men and set on fire. Tacitus is specific on British Druids: 'they deemed it indeed a duty to cover their altars with the blood of captives and to consult their deities through human entrails.[6]

In the book, *The Celts*, Gerhard Herm writes of the Celtic people:

> The inhabitants employ a very surprising and incredible custom when they want to know matters of great importance. They consecrate a human

The Dark Side of Halloween

being to death, drive a dagger into his belly, above the abdomen, and draw conclusions about events to come from the squirming of the victim and the spurting of his blood. They have been practicing this custom since time immemorial.[7]

From the writings of Julius Caesar, we have this account. In the century preceding the birth of Christ, Caesar conquered the Britons and he records very carefully the account of the DRUID PRIESTS:

All Gallic nations are much given to superstition... they either offer up men as victims to the gods, or make a vow to sacrifice themselves. The ministers in these offerings are the Druids, and they hold that the wrath of the immortal gods can only be appeased, and man's life redeemed, by offering up human sacrifice, and it is a part of their national institutions to hold fixed solemnities (Ceremonies) for this purpose.

I looked deeper to see if I could find the dates of these "fixed solemnities." I found the answer in an encyclopedia called *Man, Myth and Magic*. "The

PART 1

pagan Celts in Northern Europe held two great fire festivals each year - Beltane on the eve of 1 May and Samhain on the eve of 1 November - to mark the beginning of summer and winter."[8] So you see that Samhain, the forerunner of Halloween, was one of the days when human sacrifices were offered. It is interesting to note that when they gathered together on these pagan worship days they would meet in a grove of trees, preferably oak trees, or in a stone circle. There are many stone circles in the British Isles and in western Europe. The most famous surviving stone circle is Stonehenge, located on the Salisbury Plain in Wiltshire England. It is evident that human sacrifice was common at this ancient Druid Sacrificial Circle because within three miles of this site there are over 350 funeral mounds that contain the remnants of countless human sacrifices.

Stonehenge

PART 1

The Nimrod - Druid Connection

> And thou shalt not let any of thy seed pass through the fire to Molech, neither shalt thou profane the name of thy God: I am the LORD. Leviticus 18:21

Have you ever wondered where the heinous pagan worship rituals of the Druids originated? I have. As it turns out it goes all the way back to Nimrod, who built Babel or Babylon. He conceived a one world government model in rebellion against Jehovah-God and went about to establish a one world government in the land of Shinar (which is today known as Iraq) and institute a pagan worship system that rejected the Lord God Jehovah. The primary false god worshipped was called Baal (Syrian & Phoenician), Bel (Assyrian), Moloch or Molech (Ammonites), Ra or Re (Egyptian) to name just a few. Here is why that is important. *The American Book of Days* says,

THE AMMONITE FIRE-GOD, MOLOCH

> "Many of Halloween's customs are derived from the ancient Baal Festivals. Other customs originate

from the taking of omens from the struggles of victims in the fires of druidic sacrifices."[9]

Alexander Hislop wrote,

> "The worship of Bel (Moloch) and Astarte was very early introduced into Britain along with the Druids, the priests of the groves. From Bel, the 1st of May is still called Beltane in the Almanac; and we have customs still lingering at this day among us, which prove how exactly the worship of Bel or Moloch had been observed ... "[10]

The reference to "lingering customs" refers to Halloween.

Now, allow me to turn your attention back to Nimrod for a moment. It is important that you know that Nimrod incorporated into his worship system the grisly practice of human sacrifice an cannibalism. Hislop says,

> "the priests of Nimrod or Baal were necessarily required to eat of the human sacrifices; and thus it has come to pass that 'Cahna-Bal' (cahna meaning priest & Bal referring to Baal), the 'Priest of Baal' is the established word (cannibal) in our own tongue for a devourer of human flesh."[11]

Here's why that is important.

> "The god whom the Druids worshipped

was Baal, as the blazing Baal-fires show and ... children were offered in sacrifice to Baal."[12]

That's what Baal (Moloch) worshippers did. We know that because of what we read in the Bible in Jeremiah 19:5: **They have built also the high places of Baal, to burn their sons with fire for burnt offerings unto Baal, which I commanded not, nor spake it, neither came it into my mind.**

There is absolutely no doubt that Samhain - Halloween, was a wicked pagan worship day. It is little wonder that even today Halloween's focus is still on horror, mutilation, death, evil and the occult seeing that it is rooted in Baal worship! But, I come in contact with people regularly who protest, "That may have been true in the past, but that is not true today."

Witches have never given up Halloween! Occultists of all stripes still lay claim to the day and worship their pagan gods and goddesses on that day with demonic rituals.

What Witches, Satanists and Other Occultists Say About Halloween

So, what do those who are involved in the occult say about Halloween? Do they acknowledge that Halloween is a pagan day past and present? Consider the following -

Witch - Doreen Valiente:

"Halloween is one of the four Great

Sabbats of the witches that everyone has heard about. To witches, Halloween is a serious occasion, however merrily celebrated. It is the old Celtic Eve of Samhain. With the coming of Christianity, the Church tried to Christianize the old festival by making 1st November All Saints Day, or All Hallows as the old term was. Thus Samhain Eve became All Hallows Eve, or Halloween. But attempts to discourage the pagan celebrations were so unavailing that the festival was eventually banned from the Church calendar. It was not until 1928 that the Church of. England formally restored All Hallows Eve to its calendar, on the assumption that the old pagan associations of Halloween were at last really dead and forgotten; a supposition that was certainly premature."[13]

Witch - Margot Adler:

"All the Great Festivals of Paganism, wherever they may be found, correspond in common with the Solstices, Equinoxes, and other natural annual cycles of life. Most of these remain with us today in more or less disguised form as the so-called 'Christian' holidays of Christmas (Yule), Easter (Ostara), May Day (Beltane), Thanksgiving (Harvest Home), Halloween (Samhain) and even Groundhog's day (Oimelc)."[14]

Satanist - Anton Szandor LaVey (now deceased):

"Two major holidays, HALLOWEEN and Walpurgisnacht are celebrated by the Church of Satan."

Gothic & Vampire Cults:

I was the guest on a nationally aired TV talk show several years ago. I was speaking out against Halloween and warning of the dangers of occult practices. I was seated next to Catrina, who professed to be a vampire. After the show, we were assigned to the same limo to take us back to the airport. In our conversation it was clear that Halloween was a very important day for vampires. Also, many in the Gothic movement assemble at graveyards on Halloween for their bizarre celebrations.

The Day of The Dead:

I should note as well, that many Mexicans celebrate El Dia de los Muertos (The Day of the Dead) on October 31. Family members who have died are believed to return to their grave sites.

Voodoo:

The Voodoo Museum in New Orleans usually offers a special Halloween ritual in which people may see true voodoo rites. [16]

Followers of Crowley:

Major-General J.F.C. ('Boney') Fuller was a devotee of the heroine addicted, sex pervert, black magician and so called High Priest of Satanism in Britain, Aleister Crowley (1875- 1947). Crowley boasted of being "the wickedest man in the world" and openly despised Christ and the faith of his parents who were Plymouth Brethren. Fuller indicated that Samhain (Halloween) was an important ritual day to Crowley and his followers and it still is today.

Halloween Is A Recognized Occult Holiday

> **Ye cannot drink the cup of the Lord, and the cup of devils: ye cannot be partakers of the Lord's table, and of the table of devils.** 1 Corinthians 10:21

Halloween is a religious day but not a Christian day. Satanists, witches and other occultists will go to court for their right to perform their demonic rituals on this day. Halloween is a recognized religious Holiday. Here is proof -

A federal judge has set the wheels in motion to force a federal correctional facility in Jefferson County, Colorado to allow a prisoner to perform a Satanic ritual on Halloween. Tom McMillan of the Rocky Mountain Family Policy Council can't believe it. 'This case flies in the face of two upper Appeals Court cases, both of which held that

PART 1

Satanism is not a recognized religion and therefore the prison officials do not have to provide space and implements for the performance of a Satanic ritual.' McMillan says Judge Edward Nottingham issued a preliminary injunction allowing the ritual, even though the prisoner admits it includes a destruction ritual, in which he visualizes the death of his enemies.[17]

The Military Recognizes Halloween

A U.S. Air Force physical therapist who says she has been a practicing witch for four years won permission to take Halloween and seven other days off as 'religious holidays.' A spokesman at Lackland Air Force base in San Antonio said regulations require that Patricia Hutchins...be accorded the same freedom to express her religious beliefs as any other religious believer.[10]

The Prison System Recognizes Halloween

The Maine State Prison allowed members of a witch coven (the Coven of Dawn) to hold a two-hour service on the feast day they call Samhain (Halloween), after the Druidic festival of year's end. 'This is our time to give praise to our lord and lady for the bountiful harvest,' said the founder of the 'goddess-oriented' coven. He said that 75 inmates have been initiated into the religion since its start in 1981.[19]

Witches and Satanists love Halloween. They get a lot of media coverage around that time of year. It's good P.R. (public relations) for them because the coverage, as a rule, portrays them in a favorable light. In addition, Halloween generates interest in "the craft" and is good for recruitment purposes. As Craig Hawkins put it: "With increasing vigor, witchcraft is coming 'out of the broom closet.' Many witches are actively seeking public understanding and acceptance."[20]

Despite the public relations campaign to "sell" the public on the "virtues" of witchcraft, modern day witches and satanists still worship demon gods and goddesses, cast spells, practice bizarre and immoral sexual rituals, and certain individuals and groups offer animal and human sacrifices.

Texe Marrs, well known New Age researcher said this about the activities of witches on Halloween:

> Our own research confirms that on this unholy night [Halloween], witches' covens meet, drink, dance, spit out curses and spells, conjure up spirits, engage in sexual orgies, induct new members, and offer up animal and human sacrifices. (Witches have become expert at covering up these sacrifices by use of cremation ovens and the use of privately owned land preserves for disposal of bodies in deeply dug graves.)[21]

It is clear that Halloween is a religious celebration,

PART 1

but **not** a Christian celebration. It was and still is the holiday of witches, satanists and occultists. Read carefully the following words of a former High Priest in the Celtic tradition of Wicca - **"Halloween is purely and absolutely evil, and there is nothing we ever have or will do that would make it acceptable to the Lord Jesus."**

Owen Rachleff gives us some additional food for thought.

> Halloween can be, and to many is, a deadly serious affair. [It] originated with pre-Christian Druids or Celts in Northern Europe, who marked the year by four seasonal festivals. The autumn feast took place on November 1st. Early Christians, desiring a part in the traditional festivities, created All Saints' Day to coincide with the pagan rites. Satanists, acting true to form, reversed the Christian procedure. Because November 1st was All Saints' Day (All Souls' Day, November 2nd, memorializes the dead), Satanists established October 31st as an "All Demon's Night." As surely as the Christian martyrs and saints dominated their own holiday, so did the demons permeate the preceding evening. All Hallows' Eve predictably became a time of spells, curses, and horrors for those who did not believe, but for the Satanists, particularly the witches, it was

a joyous festival and major sabbat. So it remains in a diluted form, ironically celebrated by Christian society far more vigorously than All Saints' Day.[22]

Historically, Halloween is obviously and totally a pagan, worship day. It is still the most important unholy day for Witches, Satanists and other occultists. The Bible says,

> " ... I would not that ye should have fellowship with devils."**1 Corinthians 10:20**

In another place it is written,

> "And have no fellowship with the unfruitful works of darkness ... " **Ephesians 5:11**.

Halloween Specifics

Where did the name Halloween come from?

As I mentioned earlier, originally this Druid holiday was called "The Vigil Of Saman." In early Britain it was called Samhain, which is pronounced So-wein. When Roman Catholicism became a world political and religious power, the pagan customs were still widely celebrated. In 800 A.O. the Roman Catholic church moved "All Saints' Day" from May to November 1st. All of the "saints" who did not have a special day in their honor on the Catholic calendar were to be honored on All Saints' Day. It was also a time to pay respect to the dead by visiting their graves. The "new day" that was to replace the

PART 1

pagan vigil of the dead was called "All Hallow's Day." It soon became the custom to call the evening before "All Hallow's Eve, which was soon shortened to Halloween. The important fact to note is that the intended "Christianization" of the pagan day miserably failed. The Catholic Encyclopedia even admits it. It says:

> "The night of October 31st and the vigil of the feast of All Saints, Halloween derives its name from an older English term, All Hallow's Eve, although **its traditions derive from pagan worship. An important source of the customs of Halloween was the Druidic religion of pre-Christian Gaul and Britain.**"[23]

The name of the holiday is the only thing that has changed. Halloween still carries its pagan significance. Halloween is still an observance of death. There is no Christian significance to be found in Halloween. Jesus Christ is conspicuously absent! I can celebrate Christmas in a Christian way by celebrating the Birth of Christ. I can celebrate the Easter season in a Christian way by focusing on the atoning death, burial and glorious resurrection of Christ. What about Halloween? It is a day dedicated to idolatry, fear, death and the occult. You cannot celebrate those things to the glory of God. The Bible tells us, *Whether therefore ye eat, or drink, or whatsoever ye do, do all to the glory of God.* **1 Corinthians 10:31**

The Dark Side of Halloween

Dr. John MacArthur wrote these timely words about Halloween in his *Grace To You* newsletter in response to a listener who wrote and asked: **What is your perspective on Halloween?** He answered,

> First of all, dressing up like witches, ghosts, or goblins is incompatible with a Christian's testimony. Furthermore, many of the customs of Halloween are associated with the worst kinds of pagan beliefs and ceremonies; they are usually sinister things such as demons, witchcraft and superstition. If we as Christian parents simply disregard the unchristian aspects of such practices as mere fantasy or superstition and then encourage our children to participate in them, we run the risk of communicating the message that the spiritual battle waged by the rulers of darkness (Ephesians 6:10) is not to be taken seriously.

What is the origin of costumes?

The early origin of costumes is repulsive. On the evening of October 31st, the Druids ordered the people to put out their hearth fires. Then they built huge new year's bonfires of oak branches, which they considered sacred. They burned animals, crops and human beings as sacrifices to their gods and goddess. During this diabolical ritual the PEOPLE WORE COSTUMES made of animal heads and skins. They then practiced divination, looked for omens in the struggle of the victims sacrificed in the fires, jumped over the flames or dashed through them, danced and sang. All of this was done to frighten the evil spirits away. Further, they believed "Saman would then send evil spirits to attack people on the eve before the November 1st celebration. The only way these people could escape was by assuming disguises and looking like the evil spirits themselves."[24]

It seems to me that these "evil spirits" must also have been stupid spirits if they could be fooled by such a masquerade. Sadly, the fools were the superstitious idol worshippers who refused to glorify the true God. As a result they became *"vain in their imaginations, and their foolish hearts were darkened."* **Romans 1:21** As you can see, gross looking costumes have their source in paganism and because of this we should *...cast off the works of darkness and put on the armour of light.* **Romans 13:12.**

What is the origin of the bonfire?

According to *The Oxford English Dictionary*, the word bonfire is derived from the word bone-fire, so called because it was a great fire in which bones were burned in the open air.[25] The Druids held two main great ritual fire festivals each year when humans and animals were burned in sacrifice to their gods. One was held on Beltane (May eve, April 30) and the other on Samhain or Halloween. The next day, divination was done based on the bones

The Dark Side of Halloween

remaining. These ritual fires were called bone-fire.

What is the origin of Trick or Treat?

Now, just by chance if you had forgot-ten to dress up or could not fool the evil spirits by dressing in animal skins or other disguises, there was a way to exorcise them. People were to set out a TREAT of food and fruit, and provide the wandering spirit with shelter for the night. If the demon spirit was satisfied with your TREAT, it was believed that he would not TRICK you by casting an evil spell on you thereby causing havoc.

There is another shocking account of Trick or Treat written by a former witch, Irene Park. She says:

> The Druids in Ireland would go through the neighborhoods and countryside on the eve of October 31st to collect offerings to Satan. They would carry lanterns, bags of money, and canes with very sharp points on the ends (currently known as leprechaun staffs, good luck horns, or fairies' wands). At each house, they would demand a specific amount. If the household would not or could not give the offering (penance or treat), the Druid would

PART 1

use the cane to castrate the male human or one of their prize animals.[26]

In later years, James Napier, in his book, Holidays of Legend, says,

> "Irish farmers went house to house begging for food for their ancient gods. Good luck was promised to all who donated but threats were made against those who would not give."[27]

There is absolutely nothing in Trick or Treat that honors our Lord Jesus Christ! In fact it is a form of idol worship. One former witch who came to know Christ puts it this way -

> Trick or Treat is a reenactment of Druidic practices. The candy has replaced the human sacrifices of old, but it is still an appeasement of those deceptive evil spirits. The traditional response to those who do not treat is to have a trick played on them. When you give out Halloween candy, you are, in essence providing a sacrifice to the false gods. You are participating in idolatry.

After considering the origin of Trick or Treat, I quit giving out candy. I have no desire to reenact pagan Druidic practices, even in diluted form. It seems to me that' is exactly what you are doing when you give out goodies on Halloween. Reenacting occultic worship rituals certainly does not glorify God. Consider carefully the words of the Apostle Paul in

2 Corinthians 6:14-17:

Be ye not unequally yoked together with unbelievers: for what fellowship hath righteousness with unrighteousness? and what communion hath light with darkness? And what concord hath Christ with Belial? or what part hath he that believeth with an infidel? And what agreement hath the temple of God with idols? for ye are the temple of the living God; as God hath said, I will dwell in them, and walk in them; and I will be their God, and they shall be my people. Wherefore come out from among them, and be ye separate, saith the Lord, and touch not the unclean thing; and I will receive you."

What is the origin and significance of the Jack-O-Lantern?

According to the Encyclopedia,

"The apparently harmless lighted pumpkin face of "Jack-O-Lantern" is an ancient symbol of a damned soul."[28]

One article I was reading said that pumpkins and turnips were for much the same reason that costumes were used at one time. Superstitious people hollowed out turnips or pumpkins placing candles inside to scare evil spirits away from their houses. Another book I read says,

The candlelit pumpkin or skull...served

PART 1

as a beacon for the sabbat and as a signal to mark those farms and homes that were sympathetic to the Satanists and thus deserving of mercy when the terror of the night (Halloween) began.[29]

I certainly am not sympathetic to satanists, are you? Then why display a Jack-O-Lantern?

In more recent times, John Ankerberg says this about the Jack-O-Lantern:

> The carved pumpkin may have originated with the witches' use of a skull with a candle in it to light the way to coven meeting. But among the Irish, who, as noted, caused the popularization of Halloween in America, the

The Dark Side of Halloween

legend of 'Irish Jack' explains the Jack-O-Lantern. The legend goes: There was a stingy drunk named Jack who tricked the devil into climbing an apple tree for an apple but then cut the sign of a cross into the trunk of the tree preventing the devil from coming down. Jack forced the devil to swear he would never come after Jack's soul. The devil reluctantly agreed. Jack eventually died but was turned away at the gates of Heaven because of his drunkenness and life of selfishness. He was next sent to the devil who also rejected him keeping his promise. Since Jack had no place to go, he was condemned to wander the earth. As he was leaving Hell (he happened to be eating a turnip), the devil threw a live coal to him. He put the coal inside the turnip and has since forever been roaming the earth with his 'jack-a-lantern' in search of a place to rest. Eventually, pumpkins replaced turnips since it was much easier to symbolize the devil's coal inside a pumpkin.[30]

The folk tale is tragic! It indicates that the people knew neither the Bible nor the way to Heaven. **John 3:16** makes it clear that no one has to be outside of heaven. The verse says,

> *For God so loved the world (mankind), that He gave His only begotten Son, that whosoever believeth in Him*

PART 1

should NOT perish, but have everlasting life.

John 3 also makes it clear that if any individual refuses to trust Christ as Savior that person is condemned already. **John 3:18 & 36** says,

He that believeth on him is not condemned. But he that believeth not is condemned already, because he hath not believed in the name of the only begotten Son of God. He that believeth on the Son hath everlasting life: and he that believeth not the Son shall not see life; but the wrath of God abideth on him.

There is no roaming or wandering the earth. There are no deals that can be made with the Devil. It is either Heaven or Hell depending on what you have done with Christ. If you do not know Christ as your Savior, you are condemned already. If you have put your faith in Christ, Heaven will be your eternal home. (Look up the following passages of Scripture, **Romans 3:23; Romans 6:23; John 14:6; Ephesians 2:8-9; Romans 10:9-13**). If you have never trusted Christ as your personal Savior, why not pray and ask Him to forgive your sins and be your Savior?

What is the relationship black cats & cats in general have with Halloween?

In the 1959 edition of the World Book Encyclopedia under Halloween it says, Druid priests believed that

The Dark Side of Halloween

cats were once human beings but were reincarnated as punishment for evil deeds. Because of this they held cats sacred and involved them in their idol worship of October 31st and November 1st. This is supported by The American Book of Days, by George Douglas which says,

> "Druids believed the cat was sacred and that cats had once been changed (from being human and reincarnated) into that form as punishment for evil deeds."[31]

The link between witches and cats has been well known for centuries.

> "Even after Christianity spread to Europe...oxen were sacrificed on October 31st...and in medieval Europe, black cats [were] chosen as victims in the belief that they were witches in disguise [and] were burned on that day (Halloween)."[32]

It is plain to see that cats, particularly BLACK CATS were thought to represent EVIL. Further, they were a symbol of REINCARNATION.

Black cats are still associated with Halloween. Each year Humane Societies in many cities issue warnings to black cat owners to watch out for their pets. Additionally, the Society will not release black cats around Halloween for fear they will be mistreated or sacrificed. Their decision, in my opinion, is a wise one. I have been asked to evaluate occult sites on numerous occasions and sadly I have ·seen the remains of cats that have been sacrificed. Here is but one example.

> "Sergeant Lars Holden, yesterday told of the grisly find of dead cats with their feet nailed to the floor, encircled by candles, in an abandoned beachfront building ."[33]

If you have a dark or black cat, keep it in the house around Halloween.

What is the significance of bobbing for apples?

In A.D. 43 the Roman Empire was in solid control of the Celtic people. As a result of this control the idol worshipping Romans introduced another ceremony honoring their false gods and goddesses (particularly the festival of Pamona) to the already demoniacal Druid New Year's celebration. They would try to grasp fruit, floating in water, without the use of their hands. This is the origin of BOBBING FOR APPLES.[34]

SUMMARY OF HALLOWEEN'S HISTORY

Now you have a brief historical sketch of Halloween. Is there any doubt that Halloween is a pagan worship day? Halloween is doubtless the only day that you would even consider honoring the devil, witches, ghosts, vampires and perverse acts. Why honor Satan and his demons at all? **Deuteronomy 32:16-17** tells us that God is provoked when demons are honored and not him. *...They provoked him to jealousy with strange gods, with abominations provoked they him to anger. They sacrificed unto devils, not to God; to gods whom they knew not, to new gods that came newly up....* Halloween is a demonic worship day. We would be wise to heed Paul's admonition in **I Corinthians 10:20** where he says he does not want us to fellowship with demons or pagan practices in any way.

> *The things which the Gentiles sacrifice, they sacrifice to devils, and not to God: and I would not that ye should have fellowship with devils.*

THE HEROES OF HALLOWEEN

The Witch

> **Parents take notice - Witches are real and witchcraft is popular with teenagers today. Your daughter or son may be a witch or at least into the beliefs of witchcraft.**
>
> **According to a Gallup poll, "a majority of teenagers believe in witchcraft."[35]**

The primary "hero" of Halloween is the witch.

PART 1

Consider this material from An Illustrated History of Witchcraft:

> The witch is, without doubt, one of the most enduring figures in superstition and literature. Whether portrayed as an aged crone astride a broomstick off on some mission of evil, or else a young girl dancing naked with her companions in a wooded grove, she can be found in carvings of antiquity or the columns of today's newspapers ... since the Middle Ages, (writings have) shown her as an enemy of humanity, a solitary being able to compact with the Devil to work all manner of supernatural powers.[36]

The oldest known illustration of a witch dates back to the pre-Columbian times and shows the goddess Tlazolteolf naked, wearing a pointed hat riding a broomstick. The most famous witch in history probably is the Witch of Endor. **I Samuel 28** relates how King Saul went to her in an effort to get in touch with the dead prophet of God, Samuel. He wanted advice on

The Goddess Tlazolteolf

how to defeat the Philistines. He should have known better because **Exodus 22:18** notes that being a witch was a capital crime, punishable by death. **Deuteronomy 18:9-14** makes it clear that people are neither to consult nor participate in the OCCULT. The passage says,

> *When thou art come into the land which the Lord thy God giveth thee, thou shalt not learn to do after the abominations of those nations. There shall not be found among you any one that maketh his son or his daughter to pass through the fire, or that useth divination, or an observer of times, or an enchanter, or a witch, Or a charmer, or a consulter with familiar spirits, or a wizard, or a necromancer. For all that do these things are an abomination unto the Lord: and because of these abominations the LORD thy God doth drive them out from before thee. Thou shalt be perfect with the LORD thy God. For these nations, which thou shalt possess, hearkened unto observers of times, and unto diviner: but as for thee, the LORD thy God hath not suffered thee so to do.*
> **Deuteronomy 18:9-14**

The New Testament addresses witchcraft as well. **Galatians 5:20** and **Revelation 21:8**, in the King James version of the Bible lists the practitioners of witchcraft as fleshly sin and those who practice it

PART 1

are said to be excluded from God's kingdom. Witchcraft is serious business!

The Origin of The Name "Witch"

Many of today's witches elect to be called **"wiccans"** instead of witches. The very name **witch** conjures mental images associated with evil and they want to change that. They go to great lengths to redefine themselves by using the term **wicca**. But, the word witch comes from the Old English word **wicca** (masculine) **wicce** (feminine) which means **to practice sorcery**. In fact our English word **wicked** is from the root word **wicca** and literally means **witch-like**.[37] As early as 890 A.D. the word "wiccan" was used to identify witches "in the *Laws of King Alfred*."[38] In short, changing the name from **witch** to **wiccan** is an attempt at historical revisionism. A witch or **wiccan** is, by the very name, a defining word for wickedness.

The Influence of "the wickedest man in the world" on Wicca

So, are witches really wicked? To answer that question let me introduce Aleister Crowley (1875-1947). As I mentioned earlier, Crowley boasted of being "the wickedest man in the world" and openly despised Christ and the faith of his parents who were Plymouth Brethren. One author wrote, "Everyone knows about Aleister Crowley, of course. He was a satanist, a pornographer...a traitor to his country during the war of 1914-1918, an insatiable ambisexual athlete, a pimp who lived on the immoral earnings of his girl-friends, and a junkie who daily took enough heroin to kill a roomfull of people."[39]

The sadistic, satanic teachings of this "Beast 666" (as he called himself) are being used in a number of occult organizations including Ordo Templi Orientis, The Hermetic Order of the Golden Dawn, various satanic cults and Wicca. Indeed Crowley has had a major influence on Wicca, despite the ardent denial of many Wiccans. First, Crowley had a major impact on Sybil Leek, a well-known witch. She studied under him and boasted that Crowley's mantle was passed onto her.[40] Second, Alex Sanders (1926-1988), who was "certainly one of the most influential Wiccans of the last 25 years, claimed to have known Crowley and studied under him. He also wore a magic ring identical to the one which Crowley used to wear and casually let it be known among his friends that Crowley had bestowed it upon him."[41] Finally, there is Gerald Gardner (1884-1964). Dr. Aidan Kelly, Ph.D., a witch himself, says that <u>Gardner is the inventor of the cult of Wicca</u>. There is definite evidence that Gardner commissioned Crowley to write parts of his witchcraft work the *Book of Shadows*.

PART 1

My point is simply this, **there is nothing wholesome in contemporary witchcraft.** To be sure witches are out of the broom closet and walking down main street. Some of the more commonly known names in contemporary witchcraft include Margot Adler, Starhawk, Isaac Bonewits, Jessie Wicker Bell (Lady Sheba), Lady Sintana, Zsuzsanna (called "Z"), Budapest, Laurie Cabot, Scott Cunningham, Selena Fox, Amber K, Gavin and Yvonne Frost, Judy Kneitel (Lady Theos), Leo Martello, Miriam Simes (Starhawk), Allyn Wolfe, Doreen Valiente, Otter (Oberon) G'Zell, Morning Glory Zell and more. In fact Selena Fox, witch of Circle Sanctuary in Mt. Horeb, Wisconsin, received coverage for her pagan group in the May 6, 1991 issue of *TIME* magazine. The title of the article, was

"When God Was a Woman. "⁴²

Witches got the cover of *Milwaukee Magazine* in 1992. It says,

> "Witches: Tales and Truths. Witchcraft is alive in Wisconsin. The rituals may seem strange - to some even evil - but the beliefs will surprise you. Milwaukee witch Mary Ellen Grenda and the tools of her trade."⁴³

In fact, they are going to great lengths to sanitize their reputation and remake their image. That is easy to see when you see media articles with titles like - *Witches spell it out: Don't Stereotype Us*, and *I Am Not A Wicked Witch*. In the process of trying to remake themselves to be acceptable to mainstream Americans they use deceptive schemes, old tricks and dirty lies to accomplish their goal.

Unmasking The Truth About Witches

Witches are not the wholesome, family oriented people they claim to be. Doreen Irvine, a practicing witch for many years, said, many "witches were lesbians and homosexuals." And she's right. I have a poster, letter and application in my files for, <u>as they called it</u>, "FAGGOT WITCH CAMP." The letter advertised the "second annual FAGGOT WITCH CAMP, August 26-30, 1991." This event was held at Wyalusing State Park in Prairie du Chien, Wisconsin. According to the letter, "Our purpose in

PART 1

organizing this event is to gather with like-minded queer men and to explore our unique perspectives and experiences as faggot witches." This sodomite gathering was even announced in two prominent witchcraft publications, *Circle Network News; Spring 1991* and in *Green Egg - A Magazine of Goddess and Nature Religion*; Litha, 1991.

Witchcraft is a perverted sex oriented cult. According to the book, *What Witches Do*, "witchcraft has always been a fertility religion..." and the orgy was a part of the Craft "giving the plainer girls a chance."[44]

Gardinarian witch, Patricia C. Crowther, describes modern day witch orgies this way -

> The motives of the modern witches are often thought to be questionable, and certainly a considerable element of sexuality is present at many meetings ...The nudity of the coven, the frantic dancing, the incense and the slightly illicit atmosphere contribute to this... The binding and whipping of new initiate for 'purification' purposes, for instance, is highly titillating for those with sado-masochistic tendencies... while 'the five-fold kiss' bestowed by the high priest or priestess on the feet, knees, genitals, breasts and lips of the new members speaks for itself. The 'Great Rite,' performed at certain ceremonies and consisting of token or

actual sexual intercourse...is justified on the grounds that Wicca is, after all, a fertility cult. Only the high priest may initiate a female member, while the high priestess initiates the males. [45]

While not all occult groups practice these evil rites, it is not the exception to the rule.

The book, *People of The Earth: The New Pagans Speak Out,* includes a chapter titled **Sacred Prostitutes.**[46] A pagan who calls herself D'Vora is one of those interviewed in this chapter. She is the author of a book called *Reflections from the Orgynizor.* The book says she is known as "Queen of Thelema...the Prostitute, Sex Magician, Cat Woman and as a sacred prostitute."[47] Most of what she says is too perverse to print. Suffice it to say that she characterizes witchcraft pretty well with this sentence; **"I'd say most of magic is sex."**[48] She continues in the article to promote ritual prostitution and says, "I like group sex, I like anonomys sex, I like sex."[49] It is interesting that the Bible connects the whore, the adulterer and the sorceress. **Isaiah 57:3** speaks of the *"sons of the sorceress, the seed of the adulterer and the whore."* We are told to flee fornication, not embrace it (1 Corinthians 6:18). Sexual perversion is never wholesome! Many witches are into sexual activities that the Bible forbids.

Speaking of sexual perversion I also have in my files a copy of a witchcraft publication that states that a well-known east coast witch "transitioned

PART 1

from male to female on Samhain, October 31"[50] What that means is that the person was born a biological male but had his sex organs surgically removed and altered to appear to be female. That IS perversion! In fact, another noted witch who has authored a best-selling book on witchcraft under a female name, was born a biological male.

In 1991, I published a thirty page research report entitled, *"The Dark Side of Halloween."* In that book I quoted a former witch who said, "Sadism was practiced frequently..." That is true. Several years back I brought this up on a national talk show. When I said this, two witches who worshipped Dagon were sitting on one side of me and a vampire on the other. The audience was peppered with witches. As soon as the words were out of my mouth there was a hot protest from the witches. In fact, since the show was not live, the witches put so much pressure on the producers that they edited out my words! They did not want the public to know about their sadistic practices.

Let me lend support to my assertion about *sadism*. "One of the most important religious organizations of Neo-Paganism in America is the Church of All Worlds (CAW)...CAW played a key role in the 1970's in the networking of diverse Pagan and Wiccan groups..."[51] Their official journal is the *Green Egg - A Journal of the Awakening Earth*. The entirety of *Volume 29, No. 119; 1997* dealt with ritual sexual sado-masochism. There certainly is nothing wholesome about sado-masochism.

I will conclude this section by saying, there is nothing wholesome about any of these perverted sexual practices. While witches try to mask these diabolical practices, the record speaks for itself. And as Dr. Merill Unger observes, "for those who surrender to worship and serve Satan, the moral degradation and perversion is horrifying."

LIES WITCHES TELL

> **Ye are of your father the devil, and the lusts of your father ye will do ... he is a liar, and the father of it** John 8:44

Lie #1 - Witches Do Not Believe In or Acknowledge The Devil/Satan

While Wicca and other witchcraft traditions have a modern origin, they draw eclectically upon occult information, rituals, and ceremonies from idol worshippers of the past. In fact, they use a deceptive scheme involving semantic word games to deny their involvement with the Devil and or Satan. For instance, most witches will tell you that they believe in Lucifer. They claim that "he is the god of the Sun and of the Moon." However most knowledgeable witches recognize that the book *La Sorciere* by French historian, Jules Michelet, is a major contributor to the Wiccan cult. (The English version is published by Citadel Press under the title *Satanism and Witchcraft*) But, here's the facts. "Michelet's book is full of passionate, sympathetic depictions of Satan and medieval witchcraft. "[52]

PART 1

Then there is the book by Charles G. Leland - *Aradia: Gospel of the Witches*, which is another major source of Wiccan beliefs. The very first paragraph reads...

> Diana greatly loved her brother Lucifer, the god of the Sun and of the Moon, the god of Light, who was so proud of his beauty, and <u>who for his pride was driven from Paradise</u>.[53]

This is a reference to **Isaiah 14** in the Bible where Lucifer is expelled from the presence of God and becomes the Devil or Satan! In fact, **Isaiah 14:12** (KJV) is the only passage where Lucifer is mentioned in the entire Bible. Otherwise he is called the Devil, Satan, the Dragon, etc. But that is not the only example. In *Mastering Witchcraft: A Practical Guide for Witches*...Paul Huson makes this statement:

> This is a beginner's guide to practical witchcraft, revealing the techniques and secret workings of those who practice the black arts. It presents the first steps to becoming a witch...It answers all the basic questions about spells, magical recipes, rituals, divination, covens, curses, apparatus, how to develop one's power, etc. From reciting the Lord's Prayer backward through ... details for spells to arouse lust...attain vengeance...[54]

Speaking of vengeance, consider this ritual of

wrath "a conjuration of the Horned One" recorded on page 186 –

> "I conjure thee by Barabbas, by Satanas, by the devil cursed be! I summon thee by Barabbas, by Satanas by the devil conjured be! By the underworld itself..."[55]

Need I note that Barabbas and Satanas are references to the devil who is mentioned?

Lucifer is the devil, Satan. Their slick little word games are the attempt of modern witches to cover up the truth.

Lie #2 -The upside-down pentagram is Satanic not Wiccan

Nothing could be further from the truth! While the upside-down pentegram is used in Satanism, it is well documented that in the Gardinarian and Alexandrian Wiccan cult, they use the upside-down pentagram as the symbol of Second Degree Initiation.[56] One former Alexandrian witch stated, "As I got to the higher degrees I learned that the name of the horned god was Lucifer. I learned that the sign of the second degree was an inverted pentagram, symbolizing the horns of Satan."[57]

Lie #3 - Witches only do good Magic, Healing Magic

On numerous occasions I have been told by witches that the Wiccan Rede ("An harm none, do what ye will") and the threefold law (evil directed at another will return 3 fold upon the perpetrator) hinders witches from directing magic spells or other negative actions against anyone. That just is not true! For instance, famous witch, Sybil Leek, published a book called the *Book of Curses*.[58] It is an encyclopedia of curses that witches can use in their spells. Then there is Paul Huson's book, *Mastering Witchcraft*. In it, "full details are given for spells to...attain vengeance."[59] Obviously curses and vengeance are a part of witchcraft. This is just another attempt by witches to mask the truth.

Lie #4 - Witches don't believe in blood rituals, animal or human sacrifice

While many pagan and Wicca cult members offer fruit and vegetable sacrifices to their pagan gods and goddesses, blood rituals and animal or human sacrifices are a part of historic pagan and witchcraft rites and are becoming increasingly frequent in the witch community today.

I have read several accounts and have recorded personal testimonies of individuals who were initiated into witchcraft that incorporated rituals using their own blood. Consider Alex Sanders (1926-1988). He is the father of Alexandrian Wicca. He was initiated into witchcraft using a blood ritual.

> (A witch had) "him stand nude in a circle with his head down. She took a sharp razor, cut his scrotum to make it

bleed...He was initiated as a third degree, and he became a black magickian."[60]

There are other uses of blood as well. For instance there is a connection between blood and the witches wand. 'The most efficacious wand will be made of one of the woods sacred to the White Goddess: elderberry, willow, rowan, hazel, oak or mistletoe."[61] The article goes on to say that the branch is then hollowed out and "filled with cotton wool and brought to life with three drops of the witch's own blood."[62]

The use of blood to facilitate power is not uncommon. One witch told me that they had anointed their divination board with their own blood so as to give the board power.

In the book, *"Secrets of the Occult"* by C.A. Burland, it talks about groups in south Germany about 1960 who "hunted and decapitated deer for a blood-drinking rite."

I told you earlier that the Gerald B. Gardner is considered the originator of modern Wicca. He was involved in planning a human sacrifice. Here is what is recorded. "The group was deadly serious about their secret ritual... But to be 100 per cent effective there would have to be a human sacrifice."[63] One of the coven members volunteered to be the human sacrifice.

The coven was also known to use a

> hallucinogen. Having formed their magic circle in the depths of the forest, the group, who were naked, made a line and held hands and then danced furiously around a small bonfire, chanting incantations...They performed the rite with such vigour that one or two of them fainted, a not uncommon experience when a serious amount of power and energy is aroused by the performance of ritual. The old volunteer duly collapsed and died, and it is not known whether it was from an overdose of mushrooms, over-exhaustion or the cold. The great sacrifice had been made and the potency of their magic...enhanced...[64]

Though the group was ready to murder the volunteer, as it turned out they did not have to.

The fact is, historically, human sacrifice has been associated with witchcraft. Anyone who is intellectually honest will admit that. But it seems that some Wiccans are finally coming out of the closet and preparing the way for the acceptance of human sacrifice within their ranks. In fact, a major Wiccan periodical carried an article titled *Sacrifice: An Elevation.* In this article Nasira Alma states,

> "We cannot be 'above' sacrifice, human or other...Diviners foresaw events by noting the manner of the victim's fall, the twitching of his limbs, and how his blood spurted...Sacrifice is the law of

The Dark Side of Halloween

our nature. It maintains the balance between the inner and the outer, the physical and the spiritual, the Divine and the human."[65]

Witches desperately want public acceptance! Many will lie in an effort to get it. A massive nation wide disinformation campaign is being waged in an effort to convince people that their beliefs and practices are normal and acceptable. They are neither normal nor acceptable. Their beliefs are aberrant and their practices are wicked.

Definitions, Doctrines & Principles

The word "occult" comes from the Latin word "occultus" and means secret, concealed, hidden or esoteric (private; only understood by a select few) knowledge or practices.

> It often employs a dangerous spiritual element that is called upon at times through ritualistic means. Altered states of consciousness can be used as tool to tap into a deceptive spiritual power that resides within the normally invisible and intangible demonic sphere of" reality. Magickal seduction, psycholigical problems, predatory or belief crimes can be the end result. [66]

The Encyclopedia Britannica -Micropaedia, gives some additional information that I think would be helpful. It says the occult is:

> A general designation for various

PART 1

> theories, practices, and rituals based on esoteric knowledge, especially alleged knowledge about the world ·of spirits and unknown forces of the universe. Devotees of occultism strive to understand and explore these worlds, often by developing the [alleged] higher powers of the mind...Occultism covers such diverse subjects as Satanism, astrology, Kabbala, Gnosticism, theosophy, divination, witchcraft, and certain forms of magic.[67]

Actually, there are more than 7,000 practices known to relate to the occult and many more individuals, societies, groups and religions that promote and advocate occult practices. There are numerous directories and dictionaries of occult organizations. I am a minor contributor to the *Dictionary of Cults, Sects, Religions* and *The Occult* published by Zondervan. This is an excellent one volume work if you want to learn more about cults and occult.

WHAT DO WITCHES BELIEVE?

I have been researching the occult and witchcraft for nearly two decades now. Within that time I have found that it is impossible to say ALL witches or occult devotees believe one unified doctrinal statement because they do not. As Craig Hawkins noted in his research article entitled, *The Modern World of Witchcraft,*

> "Contemporary witchcraft is so diverse

The Dark Side of Halloween

and eclectic that it is extremely difficult to accurately identify and define."

Without a doubt his statement is true. Yet, I have found a core of recurring beliefs that most witches and occult devotees believe.

COMMON WITCHCRAFT & OCCULT BELIEFS

> Now the Spirit speaketh expressly, that in the latter times some shall depart from the faith, giving heed to seducing spirits, and doctrines of devils; Speaking lies in hypocrisy; having their conscience seared with a hot iron; 1 Timothy 4:1-2

ANIMISM - The false belief that all objects (rocks, trees, wind, plants, mountains, etc.) are alive and have a soul. Here is how this false belief is practiced by many witches. They believe that spirits inhabit everything and especially sacred sites. They call these spirits **Nature Spirits** or **Elementals**.

> The term nature spirit is used synonymously with Elementals, the beings who exist in the four Elements of earth, air, fire and water. In Neo-Paganism and neo-pagan Witchcraft, nature spirits are to be treated with respect, as they can combine into a powerful energy. Their participation and cooperation is sought to enhance rituals and stimulate communication between mankind and Mother Earth. When sites are selected for outdoor

PART 1

> rituals, an effort is made to communicate with nature spirits...to secure their cooperation and seek their guidance.[68]
>
> In working magic, Witches summon the subtle forces of the elements and their guardian spirits...(these elemental spirits) may be summoned by witches to assist in MAGIC, such as weather control. Earth elementals are known as Gnomes; Fire elementals as Salamanders; Water elementals as Undines; Air elementals as Sylphs. They may be seen by physically gifted persons who are close to nature. Some elementals are said to be malicious and unpredictable, tricking human beings into accidents, setting traps for them and killing them. [69]

By the way, do you know that Trolls (remember the famous troll dolls that were popular a few years back?) are earth spirits? The troll belongs to "the supernatural fairy community which was once assumed to exercise dominion over nature."[70] And you should also know that "the pagan goddes of Rome Diana (the virgin goddess of the hunt, moon and goddess of fertility) was the queen of all nature spirits."[71] The apostle Paul encountered great opposition in Ephesus, the center of Diana Worship (also called Artemis in the Greek). These idol worshippers hated the message of Christ! (Read Acts 19:21-41). Witches today worship the Mother·

The Dark Side of Halloween

Goddess and you will find that it is Diana/Artemis. I should note that nature spirits are what Christians know as demons!

Now, to a second view of animism that other witches hold to. To some witches...

> animism means that the Life Force is immanent within all creation. All is imbued {permeated) by the Life Force: rocks and trees, deserts and streams, mountains and valleys, ponds and oceans, gardens and forests, fish and fowl; everything from amoebas to animals to humans. All is infused with and participants in the vital Life Force or energy, and therefore the entire earth is a living organism.[72]

To them, all nature is alive and all nature is sacred. Therefore some worship nature and some worship the power, god energy or Life Force that is manifested in nature.

PANPSYCHISM - Though this is similar to animism it adds a new dimension. Panpsychism is the false belief that "all objects in the universe have an inner or psychological being and thus possess some level or kind of consciousness... some panpsychists even postulate that ever object has a soul, spirit or mind."[73] It does not matter if it is a rock or a plant. Noted witch, Starhawk holds this belief. She says, "To Witches...all things-plants, animals, stones, stars-are alive, and on some level conscious beings. All things are divine and are manifestations of the Goddess."[74]

MONISM - The false belief that views everything in the universe as being an extension of one reality. The plurality in the cosmos is derived from a single ultimate source. God, the spirit world, and creation are ultimately one in essence. All diversity, therefore, flows from a uniform and divine Force or Energy. There are no Creator-creation distinctions. All differentiation is an illusion and is absorbed into one Source, Energy or "Force" of all that exists. This absurd philosophy would go something like this - "Out of ONE has proceeded the many, and back into ONE are many traveling."

PANTHEISM - The false belief that everything is divine (god). Divinity is inseparable from and immanent in everything such as nature and humanity. This belief is the basis for the self-deification and nature (creation) worship of most occultists. The primary quest of humanity is to discover and tap into the knowledge of the divine that resides in nature and within ourselves. Most witches believe that humans are gods (goddesses) or potentially gods.

POLYTHEISM - The false belief in many deities (gods/goddess-es) and religions. This also is stretched to include belief in multi-levels of reality. There is no one way or right religion for all. "All religions are simply different, equally valid paths that lead to the same destination: realizing one's potential or actual divintiy."[75]

EXISTENIALISM - The false belief that stresses the total freedom of individuals coupled with the ability to "know" by intuition, experience and feelings. Truth is therefore subjective. "One view is as good or true as another because it is at least true for the individual. Reality, then is a matter of perspective-and everyone has a different one."[76]

RELATIVISM - The false belief that there are no absolutes in any area of life. There is no right or wrong morality, religion, etc. What is right for you is right. You are the judge. The only "absolute" is that there are no absolutes.

REINCARNATION - The false belief that the soul, upon the death of the body, moves to another body or form based on the Law of Karma. The Law of Karma is the Hindu law of retributive justice. It is the belief that the load of guilt or innocence accumulates as the result of good or bad actions committed during a person's lifetime. These accumulated actions determine one's lot in the next life. Good Karma means a good reincarnation, while bad Karma means reincarnation into a less desirable state.

Most witches believe in, invoke and worship the **Mother Goddess** and her male consort, the **Horned God**. The Mother Goddess is also known as the **Triple Goddess** because she manifests herself as maiden, mother and crone. Wisconsin witch Scott Cunningham, husband of Wisconsin

PART 1

witch Selena Fox says, "the Goddess is the female force, that portion of the ultimate energy source which created the universe."[77]

The Mother Goddess is worshipped and invoked under a variety of names: Aphrodite, Artemis, Diana, Gaia, Isis, Kali, Lilith, Luna, Venus and many other names. For instance, the popular Irish vocalist called Enya is really named Eithne Ni, after a Celtic goddess. In 1993 I covered *The Parliament of The World's Religions* for several Christian organizations. At one of the sessions, Witch Olivia Robertson invoked (prayed) to Isis and yet noted that she is known by a variety of other names. Here is her pagan prayer.

The Dark Side of Halloween

Holy Goddess Isis, mother of all beings, come to our hearts. Grant us, thy children, love, beauty, and truth. We offer thee our loving care to all who are bought of thee. In the Name of Isis of 10,000 names, may all beings be blessed. The company here assembled, the spirits all around us: human, animal, birds, reptiles, fish, insects, trees, the great rain forests, plants, the earth and all her sacred elements, Baraka![78]

The Horned God is worshipped and invoked under a variety of names: Adonis, Apollo; Cernunnos, Dionysius, Eros; Hades; Horas Lucifer; Odin, Pan, Thor, Woden and more.

None of these beliefs are Biblical. Anyone who believes them is **"giving heed to seducing spirits, and doctrines of devils."** 1 Timothy 4:1

THE QUEST FOR WISDOM & POWER

It is important for you to understand that there are **two sources of wisdom and power that mankind can access - God's Wisdom and Power** and **the Devil's Wisdom and Power**. We see this in **James 3:15-17**

> "This wisdom descendeth not from above, but is earthly, sensual, devilish. For where envying and strife is, there is confusion and every evil work. But the wisdom that is from above is first pure, then peaceable, gentle, and easy to be entreated, full of mercy and good fruits, without partiality, and without hypocrisy.

The wisdom that *"decendeth not from above"* is demonic wisdom (Lucifer's, the Devil's or the Satan's wisdom). This corrupted wisdom, is characterized as being **earthly, sensual** and **devilish**. "The wisdom that is from above," God's

Wisdom, is said to be **pure, peaceable, gentle**, etc. In short, there are two very different kinds of wisdom with two very different outcomes.

Biblical Christianity is the manifestation of God's wisdom and power from above. Witchcraft, paganism, the New Age, Satanism, etc. are manifestations of the Devil's wisdom and power from beneath.

The Means That God Approves For Accessing His Wisdom & Power

God's Wisdom and Power may be accessed through ...

PRAYER -

> *If any of you lack wisdom, let him ask of God, that giveth to all men liberally, and upbraideth not; and it shall be given him.* **James 1:5**

BIBLE STUDY & MEDITATION –

> *The law of the LORD is perfect, converting the soul: the testimony of the LORD is sure, making wise the simple.* **Psalms 19:7**

> *Let the word of Christ dwell in you richly in all wisdom; teaching and admonishing one another in psalms and hymns and spiritual songs, singing with grace in your hearts to the Lord.* **Colossians 3:16** (See also 2 Peter 3: 15-16 & 2 Timothy 3: 16-17)

PART 1

For the word of God is quick, and powerful, and sharper than any twoedged sword, piercing even to the dividing asunder of soul and spirit, and of the joints and marrow, and is a discerner of the thoughts and intents of the heart. **Hebrews 4:12**

WISE COUNSEL –

A wise man will hear, and will increase learning; and a man of understanding shall attain unto wise counsels: **Proverbs 1:5**

The way of a fool is right in his own eyes: but he that hearkeneth unto counsel is wise. **Proverbs 12:15**

How People Attempt To Access Demonic Wisdom

There are occult means that people use with the intent of tapping into demonic wisdom. But the Bible warns us that God condemns and forbids seeking after demonic wisdom. This is clearly expressed in **Deuteronomy 18:9-12** where we are told not to learn to imitate detestable demonic ways such as divination, sorcery, witchcraft, channeling, necromancy, casting spells and more because they are said to be an **abomination to the Lord.**

There are three means that occult devotees use in an attempt to tap into occult power...

DIVINATION – FORTUNETELLING

Divination is the old term and fortunetelling is the modern word. They both refer to the same occult practice. Divination is the act of attempting to prophesy (forecast future events) or human character through occult means by making use of certain omens or divination tools such as tarot cards, tea leaves, Ouija board, astrology, palmistry, crying devices (crystal balls, mirrors, crystals, etc.). The methods of divination often change but the spirit and force behind if remains the same ... **a demon spirit (Acts· 16:16-18).**

There are hundreds of varieties of divination: Catoptromancy, Hydromancy, Chiromancy, Iridology, Palmistry, Mirror Mantic, Cartomancy, Alectryomancy, Onirocriticism, Numerology, Psychometry, Capnomancy, Geomancy, Pyromancy, Tephromancy, Telenomancy and more.

PART 1

SORCERY - MAGICK

The magic that most of us are acquainted with is sleight-of-hand magic, like picking a silver dollar out of the air or pulling a rabbit out of the hat. Technically that kind of magic is called legerdemain magic. It is the art of illusion. We are **NOT** referring to that kind of magic.

Often, but not always, adherents to occult magick differentiate between their magick and sleight-of-hand magic by spelling theirs MAGIC**K**. Occult magick is technically called non-legerdemain· magic.

Sorcery or magic is the act of attempting to contact, manipulate or control people, spirits, animals, plants, the elements (earth, air, fire, water) through occult rituals, ceremonies, objects (amulets, talismans, charms, etc.) Though magic may **"work,"** the power behind magic is demonic and those who practice magic are the enemies of righteousness. Here is God's evaluation of those who practice sorcery or magic -

> *And when they had gone through the isle unto Paphos, they found a certain sorcerer, a false prophet, a Jew, whose name was Barjesus: Which was with the deputy of the country, Sergius Paulus, a prudent man; who called for Barnabas and Saul, and desired to hear the word of God. But Elymas the sorcerer (for so is his name by*

interpretation) withstood them, seeking to turn away the deputy from the faith. Then Saul, (who also is called Paul,) filled with the Holy Ghost, set his eyes on him, And said, **O full of all subtlety and all mischief, thou child of the devil, thou enemy of all righteousness, wilt thou not cease to pervert the right ways of the Lord? Acts 13:6-10**

There ae hundreds of varieties of occult magic: White Magick, Black Magick, Red Magick, Tantric (sex Magic); Blue Magick, Neutral Magick, Liturgy Magic, Sympathetic Magic, Magic Mesmerism, Magnetism, Magical Hypnosis, Lycanthropy, and many more.

SPIRITISM - NECROMANCY

Spiritism or necromancy is an occult activity grounded in the belief that through certain persons acting as mediums or channels (psychics, necromancers, channelers, etc.) the dead or the spirit world can be contacted and hidden information can be acquired from those contacted. Trances and seances are often used by the medium. The power behind this activity is demonic. This activity is forbidden by the Lord. **1 Chronicles 10:13,** *So Saul died for his transgression which he committed against the LORD, even against the word of the LORD, which he kept not, and also for ·asking counsel of one that had a familiar spirit, to inquire of it.* (**1 Samuel 28:7** gives the context).

PART 1

There are scores of different types of necromency: Seances, Telekinesis, Levitation, Apports, Spiritualistic Visions, Automatic Writing, Spirit Raps, Speaking in Trances, Spirit Photography, Materializations, Table Levitation or Tilting, Ectoplasm and more.

By their own testimonies, witches, neo-pagans, Wiccans, Satanists, New Age adherents, etc. without exception, attempt to secure their wisdom and power through one or more of the occult means I have just mentioned.

We are to order our lives by the Wisdom and Power of God. That is the wisdom and power revealed in the Bible.

> *Jesus saith unto him, I am the way, the truth, and the life: no man cometh unto the Father, but by me.* **John 14:6**

We are to reject the wisdom from beneath, the wisdom of the devil, the wisdom of Witchcraft. The wisdom of witchcraft is the wisdom of the damned ... **Revelation 21:8**

> *But the fearful, and unbelieving, and the abominable, and murderers, and whoremongers, and sorcerers, and idolaters, and all liars, shall have their part in the lake which burneth with fire and brimstone: which is the second death.*

FOUR CATEGORIES OF SUPERNATURAL PHENOMENA

Supernatural phenomena or seeming supernatural phenomena fall into one of the following four categories:

1. **MANUFACTURED**-That is, they are man-made, designed to appear supernatural, but indeed are fraudulent.

2. **PSYCHOLOGICAL**-Mind altering drugs, hypnotism, drumming, trances, etc. can induce a mental state where the mind genuine-ly perceives something supernatural has happened but in reality it did not happen. For instance, a friend of mine had surgery. I visited him after the surgery. While there, he got a frightened look on his face and shouted out, "Keep those big dogs away from me. They are coming in the window. Don't let them get me!" The fact is, we were on the 7th floor of the hospital. The window was closed. I was right there and there were NO DOGS. But, the anesthetic my friend received caused a mental reaction and I could not convince him that there were no BIG DOGS. He saw them. Some supernatural phenomena falls into this category.

3. **DEMONIC-**The Scriptures clearly indicate that Satan and his fallen angels (demons) are the "supernatural" power behind true occult phenomena and their false religious practices (See Deuteronomy 32: 16-17; Psalm 106:35-40; Acts 16:16-19; I Corinthians 10:19-21; 2 Thessalonians

PART 1

2:9-10; I Timothy 4:1). One of the devil's key tactics is to masquerade as an *"angel of light"* (2 Corinthians 11: 14-15) or servant of righteousness to help humanity, when in reality the devil and his demons are the enemy of all mankind. Though Satan and his emissaries have supernatural power, they do NOT have unlimited supernatural power and ability. **BEWARE!** DO NOT dabble in occult practices. Those who get involved in the occult get more than they bargain for!

4.   DIVINE-The Lord God Almighty, the Triune God of the Bible, in the persons of God the Father, God the Son (Jesus Christ) and God the Holy Spirit have unlimited supernatural power and ability. Further, God has an army of Holy Angels who are endowed with supernatural abilities. On rare occasions in this present age God may work through a believer to accomplish something supernatural, but most of the time in this age He works independently of human agents.

In summary, occult activities accomplish several dangerous things. First, they expose devotees to occult philosophies of demons (I Timothy 4: 1) and motivate them to seek knowledge that is forbidden by God. Second, occult activities ultimately bring the devotees into contact with the world of evil spirits or demons. Those who become involved with these spirits get more than they bargain for. Dr. Carl A. Wickland, M.D., a physician, research psychologist and acknowl-edged authority in the occult sternly warns that involvement in the occult can cause:

The Dark Side of Halloween

> Apparent insanity, varying in degrees from a simple mental aberration to, and including, all types of dementia, hysteria, epilepsy, melancholia, shell shock, kleptomania, idiocy, religious and suicidal mania, as well as amnesia, psychic invalidism, dip somania, immorality, functional bestiality, atrocities, and other forms of criminality. Further, a great number of unaccountable suicides are due to obsessing or possessing influences of.. .spirits. Some of these spirits are actuated by a desire to torment their victims.

This should not surprise anyone acquainted with the Bible. In its pages there are illustrations to these things and we are told that the Devil is a liar and a destroyer. Dr. Luke tells us what people did with their occult material when they came to know Christ as their Savior in **Acts 19:18-19**, *"Many that believed (in Christ) came, and confessed (their former evil practices) and showed their deeds. Many of them also which used curious arts brought their books together, and burned them before all men: and they counted the price of them, and found it fifty thousand pieces of silver."* A piece of silver was a day's wage back in that day. By today's standard that could have been as much as half million dollars. If you have witchcraft material, New Age, occult or satanic literature, jewelry, etc. or Halloween paraphernalia I strongly urge you to follow the instructions recorded in **Acts 19:19.**

THE HEROES OF HALLOWEEN

Vampires, Werewolves

Another classic Halloween character is the Vampire, particularly COUNT DRACULA. You will see a number of these black caped, fanged toothed monsters running around this Halloween. But, parents, there are a several things you need to know. First, history records that people really believed in vampires and werewolves. Both were associated with black magic. Second, Dracula was a real person. Third, there are an increasing number of teens and young adults into the Gothic movement and Vampirism who really drink blood!

The History of Vampires & Werewolves

The word **vampire** is from the Slavonic word **wampyr**. The early Slavs actually believed that "the vampire is actually a living corpse, which sleeps in its tomb by day, and leaves it at night to prowl in search of blood, by which means it sustains its unholy live. The Slavs call such hideous creatures of darkness **Nosferatu**, 'the undead'"[79]

A strong belief in vampires was held in Britain until the early 1800's. Vampires and their practices have

The Dark Side of Halloween

always been associated with black magic. It was believed that those who practiced black magic in their lifetime were particularly likely to become vampires after their death according to witch Doreen Valiente. In Britain, vampires were so feared that it was the old British "custom of burying the unhallowed dead at a crossroads, with a stake through the corpse's heart. The object of this practice, which was not abolished by the law until 1823, was to prevent the corpse becoming a vampire."[80] It should be noted that **"some occultists today believe vampirism to be a fact..."**[81] Further, there is a modern revival among the youth subculture to become involved in some of the practices of vampirism.

What about werewolves?

Werewolf attacking a man from a 15th century German work called The Wild Beast of Gevaudan.

The word werewolf (also spelled werwolf) is explained when you understand that the "were" in Old English meant man. Hence you have a **man-wolf** or werewolf. An acutal cult werewolfery is

PART 1

connected with the worship of Zeus Lycaus. This cult was a part of Ancient Greek worship and was known to still be in existence in 176 A.D. W.B. Crow writes:

> The idea that a human being could be transformed into an animal was widespread among ancients ... It was thought that powerful witches could do such things, and many witches were alleged to turn themselves into wild animals, particularly wolves. This is mentioned in Pliny. Sometimes it was voluntary, sometimes involuntary, the result of a curse. The phenomenon is technically called Lycanthropy which, according to derivation means the transformation of a man into a wolf and vice-versa. The worst kind of witches were thought to indulge in it, as their behavior whilst in the form of wild animals gave them means to satisfy malice.[82]

There are several things that must be pointed out at this point. **First**, many do not realize that the origin of lycanthropy is found in what God did to Nebuchadnezzar in **Daniel 4:4-16 and 31-35**. Verse 16 says, *"Let his heart be changed from man's, and let a beast's heart be given unto him ..."* For seven years, Nebuchadnezzar wandered the fields, ate grass and behaved like an animal. Now, my point is this. Satan often tries to counterfeit the power of God! Occult lycanthropy is the Devil's imitation of God's power.

Second, I know of modern day witches that go into a trance and howl at the moon and cast spell. Shamans go into a trance and turn into power animals. History records bizarre practices of the Leopard Men and Panther Men of Africa.

Third, "modern doctors regard the delusional aspect of lycanthropy as psychological in origin. **The World History of Psychiatry** (1975) explains that hypochondria could sometimes develop into lycanthropy, and gives a disturbing contemporary account of a 30-year-old patient, who fell into melancholy, then developed a monomania which made him believe that he was transformed into a wolf (lycanthropy); he fled from men and sought refuge in the mountains, where he spent the nights howling, visiting graveyards and invoking the dead."[83]

To be sure, we would consider someone mentally ill who behaved as the person in the preceding paragraph. But, people don't actually believe in the black magic aspect of werewolves do they? The answer to that is yes. Several years ago I interviewed a young man from Wisconsin who had been heavily involved in Gothic Vampirism. In his public school library, he found a book that told him what he needed to make the magical unguent to anoint himself to become a werewolf. By performing this incantation and ritual, drinking blood and performing other vampire rituals he succeeded in becoming demon possessed. He said two familiar spirits that possessed him "would give me power and the things that I wanted in life so long as I lived my life according to their rules." This man went on to tell me, "everything seemed great at the time, but in the end I know now exactly, where they were taking me and that was to Hell."

A Look At Dracula

In 1897, Bram Stoker published his now famous novel **Dracula**. Since then more than 300 movies have been produced which feature him. But, Dracula was a real person! In the book DRACULA, A Biography of Vlad the Impaler, 1431-1476, by Radu Florescu and Raymond T. McNally, we read that Dracula was a maniac monster, the Hitler of his day. During his six year rule it was estimated by a reliable source that Dracula massacred 100,000 men, women and children. And how did he impose death? Let me quote Pope Pius II who tells how he killed 40,000 of his political foes shortly before 1462.

> He killed some of them by breaking them under the wheels of carts; others, stripped of their clothes, were skinned alive up to their entrails; others placed on stakes, or roasted on red hot coals placed under them; others punctured with stakes piercing their head, their navel, breast, and what is even unworthy of relating, their buttocks and the middle of their

entrails, and emerging from their mouths.[84]

No one was excluded, not even babies. Dracula decapitated, cut noses, ears, privates and limbs. On one occasion he even nailed the turbans on the heads of some Turks because they refused to remove them in his presence.

On another occasion he saw a man poorly dressed walking by his home. He called the man into his presence and said, "Your wife is assuredly of the kind who remains idle. How is it possible, that your shirt does not cover the calf of your leg? She is not worthy of living in my realm. May she perish!" The man protested, saying that he was satisfied with her. Dracula said, "You will be more satisfied with

PART 1

another, since you are a decent and hardworking man." His wife was fetched and immediately impaled on a stake. In the meantime the new wife was introduced and carefully shown what happens to a lazy wife. The book says, "Consequently the new wife worked so hard she had not time to eat."

Let me relate one last atrocity of this warped, demonic inspired madman. Dracula devised a plan to rid society of the burden of all the country's beggars, sick, old, lame and poor. He invited them all to a feast. Little did they know that it would become a house of horror for them. He fed them well and got them drunk and then made his personal appearance and asked them, "Do you want to be without cares, lacking nothing in this world?" Naturally they all said yes! Dracula then ordered the palace boarded up and set on fire. No one escaped. Dracula was a madman. I do not want my child associated in any way with such a degenerate reprobate, do you?

Tragically, there are an increasing number of teens and young adults into the Gothic movement and its offshoot Vampirism. And I must tell you they really drink blood! I counseled a young man for quite some time that got involved in this. He had been a Bible College student, but was expelled after he was caught drinking his own blood. Another young man told me of how he and his girlfriend were into Vampirism. Part of their ritual included sex and then cutting his arm and drinking the blood. He said "the blood lust soon overpowered the desire for sex. It is a demonic craving and desire. It grows and feeds." He went on to say, "I'd see people in certain situations and wonder what it would be like to taste their blood, the saltiness of their blood."

Or consider the article in the August 9, 1998, issue of The Journal Times published in Racine, Wisconsin.

> Nelson told investigators that he heard Buck, then 39, threatening to kill himself with a wooden stake. In the room with Buck was a 16-year-old girl, identified in court documents only as Melissa J. He reported that the teen-age girl was drunk, and that Buck ... offered her a razor blade. Melissa complied making several criss-cross slashes on her inner forearm, which were 'bleeding profusely,' Nelson said. Then Buck - a severe looking man with a pale complexion, long dark hair and long sharp fingernails - sucked on the girl's arm for several minutes ... Her arms continued to bleed for about 15 to 20 minutes. The case ... was the latest in an isolated string of vampire-like events in Wisconsin and elsewhere. In Wisconsin, police have uncovered a handful of cases in the past few years in which vampire-like activities played a role in crime.[85]

Do you see the picture? Halloween is a pagan holiday. The key heroes of Halloween are diabolical

PART 1

and demented. Halloween pro-motes concepts, practices and beliefs that are neither spiritually nor 11entally healthy. In fact, that brings me to my next major point...

THE HARM OF HALLOWEEN

I will state boldly that Halloween is harmful! Here are the reasons why.

- **Many are exposed to Witchcraft and occult practices at Halloween activities**

Like many others, I got my first exposure to occult practices at Halloween parties. My first experience came at a church Halloween party at our youth sponsor's house. A group of kids went to the basement began talking about contacting the spirits and asking them to show themselves by table levitation. I had not been exposed to anything like that before. Some of them claimed that it really worked. I became uneasy and left the party. My second experience came when I attended the Halloween party of a classmate. When it came to "game" time, we went to the basement. Carol asked us all to be seated in a circle and then placed a candle in the middle. She told us to hold hands and then turned off the lights. I asked why we were doing that and she said we were going to have a seance and to call up the devil. Not me! The last person I wanted to communicate with was the Devil. I got out of there.

I can tell you that many children get their first

The Dark Side of Halloween

exposure to occult activities at Halloween. I have received communications from all over the United States testifying to that fact. In one school district a "real" Witch was brought in and told the children of the wonderful world of witchcraft including teaching them how to cast a spell. Another group of teens went on a school sponsored Halloween field trip and visited a channeler, which is nothing but a spirit medium who practices necromancy. They had a seance with the intent of contacting (channeling) the spirit of a dead movie star.

Last year I got a call from an alarmed parent. They had discovered their daughter's diary and what they read blew them out of the water. She and several of her teenage friends were planning on being baptized into witchcraft on Halloween of 1997. Obviously this was not her first contact with witchcraft, but she and her friends had been reading occult material from the school library and decided Halloween would be a good time to form their own coven. Let's move on to the next reason Halloween is harmful. Halloween is harmful because ...

- **It provides "an acceptable" opportunity for witches and other occultists to promote pagan beliefs**

From about October 1st until October 31st, witches, vampires, Satanists and other occult minions can be seen and heard on TV and radio talk shows. There will be special features on witchcraft. Newspapers and magazines with be packed with occult related articles. Americans have been receptive to this over the years. But, what happens? That brings me to my next point.

- **Children and even adults are conditioned to be receptive to occult doctrines and practices and are desensitized by the violence and death associated with its celebration**

> **I will set no wicked thing before mine eyes: I hate the work of them that turn aside; it shall not cleave to me.** Psalms 101:3

There is no better illustration of this fact than Ann Landers' column that I came across while reading a newspaper in a restaurant one afternoon. The title of her column was *Parents Must Tackle Violence*. The parent wrote:

> I heard something today that made my hair stand on end. I hope you will deal with it in your column because it is a symptom of a problem that warrants deep concern. Last October, the teacher of a fourth grade class asked her students to write a short essay on *what they would like to do most to celebrate Halloween. Eighty percent of her 9 year-olds expressed the wish to "kill somebody."* Where do children get such ideas? I believe it is fair to say that they get them from movies on TV. What are we going to do about this love of violence among the young?

The Dark Side of Halloween

> Frankly, it scares me to death. I am - Concerned in California.[86]

Now, I can almost hear some of my readers protesting, the kids were just kidding. You don't actually believe that anyone would follow through on things like that do you? In fact there are some who do! Evangelist Dave Benoit tells of a mother finding a strange diary, called "The Book Of Shadows" in her son's room. She, with fear and trembling, leafed through pages filled with satanic drawings. Then her eyes fell on these horrifying words, "Last year I stole a car at Halloween and ran over a kid and killed him. This year, at Halloween, I plan to do the same thing!" The words in his satanic diary proved to be true. He murdered a person the previous Halloween as a sacrifice to Satan.

All parents ought to be concerned. Halloween does desensitize our children by exposing them to violence, death, mutilation and gore. Not only do they expose them to it, they glorify it! I well remember the only haunted house that I have ever been in. I took a camera with me loaded with high speed film. I was shocked by what I saw. In one of the first rooms, there was a partially dismembered woman on an operating table. As I made my way along the darkened hallway a frightening mutilated man jumped out racing a electric saw and threatening to dismember me. And then, perhaps

PART 1

Meat Case in Haunted House

the most gruesome of all was a large lighted butcher's meat case loaded with very real looking bloody body parts. Listen readers, I do not think that is funny at all. I spent several years on a fire department rescue squad and dismembered and mutilated people have never amused me. And why should it be acceptable at Halloween? Did you laugh and joke on July 22, 1991, when you heard the news that police discovered 17 mutilated and dismembered bodies· in apartment #213 which was occupied by Jeffery Dahmer? What are we telling our children if we accept that kind of scene on Halloween and yet gasp with true horror when murder-mutilations come to light on the news?

Halloween is desensitizing our children by its glorification of violence, death, mutilation and gore. Standard television and video viewing fare this Halloween will be slasher/horror movies like· Dracula, Scream, "Nightmare on Elm Street", "Halloween", and "Friday the 13th" film series and others. Jeffery Dahmer's favorite was the **Exorcist II.**

> (He) "watched this movie on almost a weekly basis, for approximately six months, and sometimes 2 and 3 times a week. He identified with the main character in the movie because he appeared to be driven by evil. Tracy Edwards (one who escaped from Dahmer) testified that Dahmer forced him to watch this video. He said that Dahmer identified with the possessed former preacher and he wanted to be demonized. Edwards went on to say that Dahmer began to chant, rocking back and forth. While he did this, it seemed like he was not even there. "[87]

Are you wondering why I am bringing Dahmer into this picture? I'll tell you why. Many of the horror/slasher pictures are inspired by incidents like the Dahmer case and Dahmer was inspired by a demonic horror picture. I should say, that this is not just my "wild speculation." Consider actor (and I use the term loosely) Robert Englund. He portrayed razor fingered, mass murderer Freddy Krueger in the "Nightmare on Elm Street" series. Where do you suppose he got his inspiration to play his part? He drew his inspiration from the late Ted Bundy, who raped, brutalized, mutilated and murdered more than 28 women. Englund told Slaughterhouse magazine, "I just read an article on Ted Bundy, so a lot of my imagery is based on him."

I have had parents and media people tell me that

PART 1

TV does not have any influence on people. Do you believe that? In fact that's bunk! Companies do not pay millions of dollars to air their commercials during Super Bowl Sunday or the Olympics because they do not influence anyone!

Syndicated columnist George Will does not believe that! He says that studies prove that "a 14-month-old infant can adopt behavior it has seen on television."[88] He goes on to say that young children are unable to distinguish fact from fantasy, and that they regard televi-sion as information about how the world works.

Harriet Kozkoff does not believe that either. This public TV producer told the press:

> Entertainment is a powerful socializing agent in contemporary society. Slasher and horror movies ...use violence and sexual arousal to maximize profits and are an inevitable prescription for conditioning sexual sadism into our pre-teen, teenage and young adult film fans.

Psychiatrist Dr. Thomas Radecki does not believe that television is neutral either. He said,

> "Every year film violence and real-life violence continues to get worse. We must protest and stop this growing sadism in our homes, schools, and on our streets."

Obviously, the problem is wider than just on

The Dark Side of Halloween

Halloween. But television programming and video rentals that feature gory, sadistic, demonic, bloody, violent themes are at their peak at Halloween.

Halloween conditions children and even adults to be receptive to occult doctrines and practices and desensitizes them by the display of violence and death.

- **Fear can have detrimental effects on people**

Fear hath torment 1 John 4:18

Fear can have adverse effects. Sometimes the effects can be momentary and at other times they can be long lasting. Here are some examples.

A Christian organization, which works with young pe9ple, planned a haunted evening for teens,. More than 550 attended. One woman sponsor became so frightened that she wet her pants. What was just as disgusting was that the organization's newsletter even reported the embarrassing incident to all of its constituents. Let me quote directly:

> Over 550 attended the event and there were over 45 salvation decisions. It has been reported to me by very reputable sources that one leader, who will remain nameless, was so scared by a certain individual with a chain saw that she had to endure wet pants the

PART 1

rest of the evening.

What's going on? Wouldn't you be frightened if, unexpectedly, a man came at you with a chain saw buzzing! I would. And if I wet my pants from the fright, I certainly would not want someone to publish it for all to read. My point is simply this, when it comes to Halloween, many Christians have set aside their discernment.

It gets worse. An article in the *Milwaukee Journal*, entitled *"Haunted House Fun: It could become a nightmare for kids"* stated, "It's just for fun, you know that. But to a young child, a trip through a "haunted house" created for Halloween could be a nightmare." Psychologist Marvin Berkowitz of Marquette University said, "Some haunted houses can frighten an adult." He warned that a child must "go in with the right mental set." He said, "Make sure they know it's going to be a fun scare, not a real scare." The article went on to say, that even though you do your best to let the child know this, he still may be traumatized by such an experience.

I don't believe children should be exposed to such manufactured traumas. Why? Because exposing a vulnerable child can have harmful consequences that run the spectrum from nightmares to emotional damage. In fact, Dr. Grace Ketterman, M.D. says in her book, *You and Your Child's Problems:*

> A tragic by-product of fear in the lives of children as early as preadolescence

is the interest and involvement in supernatural occult phenomena.

I have been counseling in this area long enough to tell you that what Dr. Ketterman says is true! What kids need is not an exposure to horror and violence. What they need to experience is the love of Christ, the love of mom and dad. The apostle John wrote,

> *"There is no fear in love; but perfect love casteth out fear: because fear hath torment. He that feareth is not made perfect in love."* **1 John 4: 18**

The final reason that Halloween is harmful is because ...

- **It provides the opportunity to experiment with the occult to see if it works and an excuse to do evil**

Many who are curious about the occult, experiment with occult rituals and practices at Halloween. Some of those who were "just playing around" get hooked. Ouija boards, seances, casting spells and small animal sacrifices are among the most common avenues of experimentation.

Others cannot wait for Halloween. They believe it is the most powerful occult day of the year. Jack Roper, occult researcher with C.A.R.I.S. (Christian Apologetics: Research & Information Service) says " ... the time of the year where you have the highest rate of satanic ritual crimes is Halloween." He went

PART 1

on to say, "Around Halloween, one of the things you see is graveyard desecration." Self-styled Satanists use human bones in their rituals. Graveyard vandalism is a common occurrence at Halloween.

A Milwaukee county parks and recreation employee contacted me several years back. He told me that he found the remains of small animals that had been sacrificed in area parks around Halloween. It was clear that these sacrifices were occult related because the remains were associated with either an altar inside a circle, triangle or pyramid structure.

Just last year a frightened woman called an associate of mine and asked us to come to her house. When we arrived she described an occult ritual that she and her daughter had seen from their upstairs window complete with hooded figures, fire, and an animal sacrifice. It took place in her neighbor's yard.

While deer hunting in Marinette County, Wisconsin, I came across the remains of a bull that had been sacrificed within a stone circle. Most likely this was part of a Halloween ritual sacrifice performed by a satanic group.

I well remember the shock and trauma caused when a Christian care facility discovered that several of the residents had been ritually abused in occult rites two years in a row at Halloween. I counseled with one of those who had been sexually abused. How could such a hideous thing ever happen at a Christian facility you may ask? The occult group was able to infiltrate the organization when one or more of their members were hired as houseparents. Through carefully planned deception, occult members slipped in and forced some residents to participate in their perverted Halloween demonic worship rituals. Residents were threatened with horrible reprisals if they breathed a word of what happened to anyone. Thankfully, after a second year of Halloween ritual abuse someone talked. The Christian organization moved quickly and brought in the police. After a careful investigation only one was prosecuted, though several were fired. But there were no convictions. The occultists got off scot-free. Those that were abused were left to deal with their physical and mental scars.

In my efforts to expose the dangers of Halloween and the other occult holidays I have been asked to evaluate many ritual sites and evaluate photos to give my opinion as to whether they are occult related. I have envelopes full of pictures of animals that have been sacrificed, graves that have been desecrated, living persons whose bodies have been mutilated in occult rituals by tattooing, cutting, piercing, whipping and branding. And then there is the envelope marked pictures of human sacrifice. There is not the least doubt in my mind that Halloween is the Devil's celebration, packed with evil!

Let's review. Halloween is harmful because ...

PART 1

1) Many kids are exposed to Witchcraft and occult practices at Halloween activities.
2) It provides "an acceptable" opportunity for witches and other occultists to promote pagan beliefs.
3) Children and even adults are conditioned to be receptive to occult doctrines and practices and are desensitized by the violence and death associated with its celebration.
4) Fear can have detrimental effects on people.
5) It provides the opportunity to experiment with the occult to see if it works and an excuse to do evil.

Where The Occult Will Lead Its Followers

There is no doubt that Halloween is rooted in the occult. Neither is there any doubt where the occult will lead those who follow. The occult will lead you into...

Idolatry - You will worship other gods and goddesses, which the Lord God of Heaven forbids. "Modern and ancient witchcraft is a nature-based, pantheistic religion...The god of the hunt and the goddess of fertility were its primary deities." I might add, they still are. Worshipping anything or anyone else is an affront to almighty God. Just read the first two of the Ten Commandments found in **Exodus 20:3-5**.

Immorality -Perverse, sexual immorality abounds within a variety of occult groups. Regardless of the

The Dark Side of Halloween

"wholesome" picture witches try to paint, their worship is rooted in pagan fertility rituals and ritual prostitution. I well remember reading the account of photographer Serge Kordiev. One of the modern definitive works on the occult, found in most good libraries, is an encyclopedia titled, *Man, Myth and Magic*. Serge Kordiev was the main photographer for that work. After he had written an article in a Sunday newspaper describing his interest in the occult, he received a telephone call from a man who asked whether he would be interested in joining a witch coven. He said yes. By appointment, Serge and his wife were picked up in an expensive car and driven to a large old house. After being given drinks at a bar they were told to strip naked and put on small black satin aprons. They were taken into a large room with a black floor and red carpets hanging on the walls. Half a dozen. hooded figures stood in front of an altar. A naked man, his body gleaming with oil, appeared before the altar. Two black-hooded girls stood on either side of him. The Kordievs were ordered to kneel, to swear perpetu-al homage to Satan, and to sign their oaths in blood. They were given magical names, and the naked man placed his hand on their genitals. After several meetings the Kordievs began to have second thoughts about the coven. On one occasion a young girl was accused of betraying the group's secrets. She was humiliated before the group and made to serve as a human altar while a Black Mass was said over her, after which she was raped by the Master. When the

Kordievs discovered that they still had to go through a 'confirmation ceremony' which involved sexual intercourse with the Master and with a High Priestess, they decided to leave the group. Almost immediately they began to have troubles, including having their photo studio broken into and trashed.

I have personally talked to others who have been forced into illicit sexual rituals that cover the spectrum from oral contact to sodomy. The Bible calls us to sexual purity. Sexual contact and sexual relationships are only to take place within the context of marriage between a male husband and a female wife. (See Exodus 20:14; 1 Thessalonians 4:3; Leviticus 18:22-23)

Injury - I have a file folder filled with articles and pictures that relate to injuries that are the result of occult rituals.

Branding - "A self-avowed Satan worshipper is jailed in Crawford County on charges that he burned an inverted cross onto a 15-year-old boy's chest. The burned youth was examined by a doctor, who described the wound as a third-degree burn."[89]

Cutting - "A 14-year-old girl was found cowering on her bed after participating in a satanic ritual involving sexual assault and mutilation. A razor blade was used to carve symbols ... into the girl's thighs, police said. Satanic symbols were painted on the floors and doors of the house. Pages of the family Bible were torn out and knives and candles were arranged in what police said was a ritualistic manner."⁹⁰

Piercing - Tongues, cheeks, noses, eyebrows, navels, lips, nipples, sex organs, etc. are all targets for voluntary or forced piercing rituals, not to mention ritual tattooing. It is important to note that cutting and piercing is pagan in origin. Baal worshippers cut themselves in pagan rituals as we see in **1 Kings 18:28**. God tells his children that they are not to cut themselves, which would include piercing. **(Jeremiah 16:6)**. The only exception I find is that women are allowed pierced ears (but not noses, navels, nipples, etc.) **(Ezekiel 16:12)**. Our body belongs to the Lord and we are not to harm it **(1 Corinthians 6:19-20)**. Brands, cuts, tattoos and pierces (except a woman's ears) are indicators of pagan ownership.

Degradation & Torture - Over the nearly two decades I have been a Biblical counselor, I have worked with numerous teens and adults who were required, as a part of their initiation, to participate in horrendously degrading activities. One woman told me she was required to spend the night cinched up in the gutted carcass of a horse and was "reborn" into the coven group the next morning. Another told of having to drink a mixture of blood, semen and urine as part of the initiation. Another was whipped over every inch of her torso. Then there is the case of Thadius, who walks with a limp today. That is because an occultist "popped" the bones in the boy's legs to punish him for trying to

PART 1

escape "two hellish days of torture by a teenage neighbor who has pleaded no contest to trying to kill the boy by methodically breaking his bones. When both legs were broken, Thadius was forced to stand over a board painted with satanic symbols and '666,' the numbers that are said to identify the anti-Christ. "[91]

Insanity - Occult involvement warps and twists your mind. Several years ago, I was called upon to visit a person who was in the psychiatric ward. As I began to talk with this teenager, I discovered that he was into the occult. He started out just dabbling in the occult, but then was irresistibly drawn deeper and deeper into it. He began hearing voices and obeying them. The voices told him to tear up his Bible and he obeyed. The voices told him to harass his younger siblings and he obeyed. The voices told him to get four knives and kill his family. He purchased the knives and carefully labeled them with the names of his mother, father, brother and sister. He was waiting for the right opportunity to obey the voices, but thankfully his mother came in to clean his room and found the knives. That's why he was in the hospital. Another pastor and I had the opportunity to show him his sinfulness and need of Christ. Right there in the psychiatric ward this teenager repented of his sins and trusted Christ as his personal Savior and was born again.

I warn you. Dabbling with the occult often leads to demon possession. And today, the possessed person often lands in a mental hospital. In our day the medical world does not recognize demon possession, but categorizes these people as having psychiatric problems. If you want a Biblical glimpse into the world of demon possession read **Mark 5:1-15**.

Suicide - I have personally talked to Steve Taylor. His step-son Dereck got involved in the occult. "Early on the evening of February 5, Dereck, 16, phoned his girlfriend, Tara, while his parents were out and told her that on the previous night he had been visited by Satan, appearing in a blue light and demanding his soul… he went to his parent's bedroom and fetched his stepfather's hunting rifle … carried the rifle down to his bedroom in the basement… put the rifle's barrel into his mouth and fired." [92] The article goes on to say, "For the Taylors, their son's death was the culmination of four months of growing alarm about his involvement in satanic worship. Indeed, last October the couple confiscated black candles, a large hand-drawn pentagram-a five-pointed star-shaped symbol alleged to have magical powers-and instruction books that, Dereck had told his mother, he had used to conduct satanic rituals."[93] Occult connected suicides are all too common. That does not surprise me since Satan is the destroyer. God warns,

> ***But he that sinneth against me wrongeth his own soul: all they that hate me love death***. *Proverbs 8:36*

PART 1

Homicide - Occult involvement too often leads to murder. I well remember listening to a woman who claimed to have been forced to participate in the ritual murder of a teenage girl. Or, consider the case of professed Wiccan, Damien Wayne Echols. He was involved with the brutal ritual murder of Michael Moore, Christopher Byres and Steve Branch. There are those who accused Echols of being a Satanist, but Echols asserts that he is a Wiccan. In a search of his home, they found a book of spells, potions and prayers which was his book of shadows. It begins with an entry stating "all rites are to be performed within a nine-foot circle." The article goes on to say, "following that, there is a ritual to be used for 'improving' the memo-ry,' which includes using the 'heart, eye or brain of a lapwing or plover (birds) and hanging it on one's neck."[94] He moved from killing animals to killing people. The Sixth Commandment is clear -**Thou shalt not kill. Exodus 20:13**

> PLEASE LISTEN! THIS IS WHERE OCCULT INVOLVEMENT WILL LEAD: IDOLATRY, IMMORALITY, INJURY, DEGRADATION. INSANITY. SUICIDE. HOMICIDE.

Read the words of Jesus Christ –

> *I am the door: by me if any man enter in, he shall be saved, and shall go in and out, and find pasture. The thief cometh not, but for to steal, and to kill, and to destroy: I am come that they might have life, and that they might have it more abundantly.* **John 10:9-10**

In conclusion, an increasing number of people are realizing that Halloween is a pagan worship day. It is a day that honors false gods and goddesses, demons and Satan. I have neither the desire to honor, enter into the worship of false gods, nor honor the devil, do you? I hope after considering the material presented that you WILL NOT CELEBRATE HALLOWEEN. Put **Ephesians 5:11** into practice,

> " ... have NO fellowship with the unfruitful works of darkness, but rather reprove (expose) them."

Christ Honoring Alternatives

> **Be not overcome of evil, but overcome evil with good.**
> Romans 12::21

I have come to the conviction that Halloween cannot be celebrated to the glory of God. Since I do believe in the principle of replacement spoken of in **Romans 12:21**, we have replaced the celebration of Halloween with something completely unassociated with it. We make it a family night and do something special as a family. But, what about churches? What should they do? If you belong to a Protestant Church I suggest you have a gathering focused on Reformation Day, for it was on October 31, 1517, that Martin Luther nailed his 95 theses on the Castle Church door in Wittenberg. There are many good videos available on the Reformation, and the History of the English

PART 1

Bible. Our office carries several titles that relate to our English Bible Heritage. Whatever you do, be sure to carefully choose the activities that will glorify God.

> **Ye that love the LORD, hate evil.** Psalms 97:10

PART 2

THE BEWITCHING OF AMERICA

The Pilgrims brought their Geneva Bibles with them when they came to this continent in 1620. They established a society that was biblically based, of that there is no doubt. The laws they established were based on God's Laws, as revealed in the Bible. This Bible basis of American culture is called the Judea-Christian Ethic. That simply means that our culture is built on Old Testament and New Testament principles. It is common practice today to ignore and even deny the biblical basis of our culture. But, those who will take the time to search the older books that were used in educating, will discover that our nation does have a biblical basis. However, most modern history books have followed the "politically correct path" of revising history, deleting references to our nation's Christian heritage.

I have a copy of The New-England Primer from 1777 that was used to teach children to read. Look carefully at the rhymes used in teaching the A-B-C's. They all are Bible centered!

A - In **A**dam's Fall, We sinned all.
B - Heaven to find, The **B**ible Mind.
C - **C**hrist crucify'd, For sinners dy'd.
D - The **D**eluge drown'd, The Earth around.
E - **E**lijah hid, by Ravens fed.
F - The judgment made, **F**elix afraid.
G - As runs the (hour) **G**lass, Our Life doth pass.

The Dark Side of Halloween

H - **H**eart, Must never part.
I - (Not included in this edition)
J - **J**ob feels the Rod -Yet blesses GOD.
K - Proud **K**orah's troop Was swallowed up.
L - **L**ot fled to Zoar, Saw fiery Shower On Sodom pour.
M - **M**oses was he Who Israel's Host Led thro' the Sea.
N - **N**oah did view The old world & new.
0 - Young **O**badias, David, Josias All were pious.
P - **P**eter deny'd His Lord and cry'd.
Q - **Q**ueen Esther sues And saves the Jews.
R - Young pious **R**uth Left all for Truth.
S - Young **S**am'l dear, The Lord did fear.
T - Young **T**imothy Learnt sin to fly.
U - (not included)
V - **V**ast I for Pride, Was set aside.
W - **W**hales in the Sea, GOD's Voice obey.
X - **X**erses did die, And so must I.
Y - While **Y**outh do cheer Death may be near.
Z - **Z**accheus he Did climb the Tree Our Lord to see.

In my search of early history books, I have found a plethora of statements made by our "founding fathers" that attest to the truth that our nation was founded upon the principles of the Bible and Christianity. Consider a few of these statements ...

George Washington – It is impossible to rightly govern the world without God and the Bible.

Benjamin Franklin - We have been assured, Sir, in the Sacred Writings that except the Lord build the house, they labor in vain that build it. I firmly believe this; and I also believe that without His concurring aid, we shall succeed in this political building no better than the builders of Babel.

Thomas Jefferson - The Bible is the cornerstone of liberty. A student's perusal of the sacred volume will make him a better citizen, a better father, a better husband.

Patrick Henry - It cannot be emphasized too strongly or too often that this great nation was founded, not by religionists, but by Christians, not on religions but on the Gospel of Jesus Christ.

James Madison - The Christian religion, in its purity, is the basis and the source of all genuine freedom in government. I am persuaded that no civil government of a republic form can exist and be durable, in which the principles of Christianity have not a controlling influence. We have staked the whole future of American civilization, not upon the power of government, far from it. We have staked the future of all our political institutions upon the capacity of mankind for self-government; upon the capacity of each and all of us to govern ourselves, to sustain ourselves according to the Ten Commandments of God.

John Jay, 1st Supreme Court Justice -The Bible is the best of all books, for it is the Word of God and teaches us the way to be happy in this world and in the next. Continue therefore to read it and to regulate your life by its precepts.

Noah Webster -Education is useless without the Bible. The Bible was America's basic textbook in all fields. God's Word, contained in the Bible, has furnished all necessary rules to direct our conduct.

Daniel Webster - If we abide by the principles taught in the Bible, our nation will go on prospering and to prosper; but if we and our posterity neglect its instructions and authority, no man can tell how sudden a catastrophe may overwhelm us and bury all our glory in profound obscurity.

The original paradigm for this nation was the Biblical model. But there has been a spiritual paradigm shift, which began slowly after WWII, but has now exponentially gained influence until it has gained predominance. **Our nation has moved from a biblical model of spirituality to a pagan model of spirituality.**

When I started doing my **Dark Side of Halloween** seminars seventeen years ago, many people were skeptical when I told them that we were in the process of a spiritual paradigm shift moving from the Biblical model to the pagan model of spirituality. Most people did not see the occult as a problem in our culture. Halloween and pagan spirituality was just a one day issue to most people. But all that has changed. We are exposed to occult teachings and practices the other 364 days a year, not just at Halloween! America has been bewitched and I believe it all started with Halloween. **Acts 8:9-11** says,

PART 2

> *There was a certain man, called Simon, which beforetime in the same city used sorcery, and <u>bewitched the people of Samaria</u>. giving out that himself was some great one: To whom they all gave heed, from the least to the greatest, saying, This man is the great power of God. And to him they had regard, because that of <u>long time he had bewitched them with sorceries</u>.*

Americans are like the people of Samaria and Halloween is the Sorcerer. Now verse 11 has come to pass. To paraphrase this verse -"To Halloween they had regard and now we have been bewitched with sorceries." America has been bewitched by the Dark Side of Halloween. Pagan spirituality is now practiced openly and commonly accepted by many, if not a majority of Americans. As a result, our nation is like the Galatians, who were so bewitched that they ignored and disobeyed the truth of Christ. **Galatians 3:1** says:

> *O foolish Galatians,* **(Americans)** *who hath bewitched you, that ye should not obey the truth, before whose eyes Jesus Christ hath been evidently set forth, crucified among you?*

Today, the truth of God is not obeyed in our culture to a large degree. In fact, it has been out and out rejected. God has been kicked out of our public schools. Prayer was the first thing to be expelled.

The Dark Side of Halloween

Next, biblical sexuality was kicked out of school, because the powers that be, considered teaching abstinence old fashioned. Nativity scenes have been removed from the public square. Now the Ten Commandments are coming off the walls of the school and courtrooms of the land. But, do you know what happens when God's truth is rejected? When the truth of God is rejected, there is a moral vacuum. And nature abhors a vacuum. Something is always substituted for God's truth and what do you think it is? It is the devil's lies! Consider **1 Timothy 4:1-2:**

> *Now the Spirit speaketh expressly, that in the latter times some shall depart from the faith, giving heed to seducing spirits, and doctrines of devils; Speaking lies in hypocrisy; having their conscience seared with a hot iron.*

Our culture is bewitched by occult doctrines and practices. Americans are filling the spiritual void in their lives by listening to demon spirits and believing demonic philosophies. Let me show you how the spiritual vacuum is being filled. Since prayer has been expelled from our public schools, millions of Americans educated in those public schools, have turned from prayer and Bible study, to "gifted psychics" for wisdom and direction for their futures. Psychics use the demonic practice of divination and necromancy to get their wisdom. Multiplied millions of dollars are spent on millions

PART 2

of calls made by Americans to their *"Psychic Friends."* In fact, Robert L. Citron, treasurer of Orange County California, regularly consulted his "gifted psychic friend" for advice on how to invest Orange County California funds. And he followed his psychic's advice but was fired after he lost 1.64 billion dollars!

Even the First Lady, Hillary Clinton, has a psychic friend named Jean Houston. Through the forbidden practice of necromancy, Hillary has had long conversations with Eleanor Roosevelt, rather, with the demon who is pretending to be Mrs. Roosevelt.

Americans have been bewitched. If you doubt it, contact Logos and ask for my book *Angels, Angels, Everywhere - But Beware!* Americans are being deceived on every hand by the New Age celestial quackery that is such a popular theme in books and magazines recently. Here is just one example of the occult New Age teachings that Americans are accepting as "gospel truth." A December 1995 *Life Magazine* article tells this lie -

> ...among vast numbers of people who yearn for spiritual growth are many who feel alienated from traditional avenues of worship. They are uncomfortable fearing God, and they are drawn to the comfy, pliable nature of the 1995 angel: a kind of God Lite. Angels help us with things God can't because he's too high up.

The Dark Side of Halloween

In his book, *Where Angels Walk*, author Thomas Anderson unveils the occult "God Lite" angles that are mentioned in the Life article. He says,

> "Angels are a gateway to spirituality for people who find the Judea-Christian image of God too threatening."[1]

Americans are bewitched! They have rejected God's truth and have believed the devil's lie. The "angelic theology" being promoted today is wildly unbiblical and from the pit. To believe that one can be spiritual, yet navigate around God, reject His Word and ignore His Christ is to fall into the trap of an angel, an evil angel...Satan. The Bible warns us of:

> *...false apostles, deceitful workers, transforming themselves into the apostles of Christ. And no marvel; for Satan himself is transformed into an angel of light. Therefore it is no great thing if his ministers also be transformed as the ministers of righteousness; whose end shall be according to their works.*
> **2 Corinthians 11:13-15**

Our nation is losing the blessing of God! I believe that the main reason this is true is because many Americans have turned their backs on our nation's biblical roots. The blessing of God is only on those nations who claim Him as Lord. **Psalms 33:12** declares: *Blessed is the nation whose God is the LORD.*

PART 2

We must reject the new model of spirituality, the devil's model and be like the New Testament Bereans. Luke wrote,

> *These were more noble than those in Thessalonica, in that they received the word with all readiness of mind, and searched the <u>scriptures daily, whether those things were so</u>.* **Acts 17:11**

Later in this book I share Bible guidelines for determining what is acceptable and what it not. Be sure to read that section.

THE PROBLEM WITH MYTHS

Another way our culture is being bewitched is by myths! Myths have their origin in pagan religions. When God's truth is rejected, myths and fables fill the void. **2 Timothy 4:3-4** says:

> *For the time will come when they will not endure sound doctrine; but after their own lusts shall they heap to themselves teachers, having itching ears; And they shall <u>turn away their ears from the truth, and shall be turned unto fables.</u>*

Myths are dangerous! Yet many people don't seem to think that they have to worry about the influence of myths. However, they should! Why? Because **the Bible warns us about the danger of myths and fables.**

Just recently I purchased the *American Dictionary*

of the English Language by Noah Webster. This is an exact reprint of his first edition of 1828. I often go back to the old books I have in my library because they have not been edited to come in line with the "politically correct" apostasy of our day. This dictionary was the first place I looked as I began my research on mythology. This is the definition for mythology...

> **"A system of fables or fabulous opinions and doctrines respecting the deities which heathen nations have supposed to preside over the world or to influence the affairs of it."**[2]

Myths or fables are based on doctrines that relate to heathen or pagan religions! That should make us sit up and take notice.

The Bible & Mythology

Does the word **"myth"** appear in the Bible? If you were to read the King James Version of the Bible you would not find the English word myth **but you should not conclude that the Bible does not address the issue**. In reality the word fable, a synonym of the word myth, occurs five times in the New Testament. Each time the word occurs the underlying Greek word is **"muthos"** from which our English word "myth" comes.

Now, what does this biblical word "muthos" mean? Strong lexicon says the word means **"a tale, i.e.**

PART 2

fiction (myth): fable." Another adds, a myth is "that which is fabricated by the mind in contrast to reality." In fact, in the New Testament, the primary use of this word denotes **"a fable full of falsehood and pretenses."** Zodhiates *Word Study Dictionary* indicates that the source of myths is from "the kingdom of darkness and lies," that is Satan's kingdom.

What does the Bible say about mythology?

- **Myths are substitutes for the truth**

We have not yet defined **truth. Truth is "the quality of being in accordance with experience, facts, or reality; conforming with fact; agreement with a standard."**[3] The standard that Christians are to use is the Bible. It is the foundation for what we believe. The Bible is our standard of truth. That's why we are to study the Bible **(2 Timothy 2:15)**. Studying God's Word is beneficial **(2 Timothy 3:16-17)** because the Bible reveals to us –

> What's right
> What's not right
> How to get right, and
> How to stay right.

But, when people reject the truth of God as revealed in the Bible something happens. **2 Timothy 4:24** tells us about it. It says:

> *"Preach the word; be instant in season, out of season: reprove,· rebuke,*

exhort with all long-suffering and doctrine. For the time will come when they will not endure sound doctrine; but after their own lusts shall they heap to themselves teachers, having itching ears; And they shall turn away their ears from the truth, and shall be turned unto fables."

This passage of Scripture reveals at least **four things about those who refuse to adhere to biblical truth** as their standard ...

1. **They are intolerant of the truth**...they will not **endure** sound doctrine...The word **"endure"** means to tolerate or put up with. They will **not** tolerate sound teaching!

2. **They make themselves the authority**... after their own lusts...This portion of the verse points out the fact that they evaluate truth based on their own selfish longings or desires. They set their own standard, they are their own authority, they are "god" deciding for themselves what is good and what is evil. Actually, making yourself the standard of measure is adopting the lie that Satan sold to Eve in Eden **(Genesis 3:4-5)**. **BEWARE!** Truth is not relative! **Psalm 119:89** *"For ever, O LORD, thy word is settled in heaven."* This verse simply says, God has preserved His unalterable standard. That standard is recorded in Heaven where man can't change it. People may try to add to, subtract and manipulate the truth here on earth, but God's standard is secure and man will be

PART 2

judged according to God's pure, permanent standard!

3. **They look for others who will support their error**...*they heap to themselves teachers, having itching ears;* It is important to realize that a majority vote does not determine truth, though it may determine whether that truth is accepted. That's where the term "politically correct" comes in. "Political correctness" is determined by "the powers that be." Those powers manipulate the truth and substitute lies based on their philosophical mind set. Those who jump on the bandwagon are "politically correct!"

4. **They substitute myths for the truth** ...*they shall turn away their ears from the truth, and shall be turned unto fables*. It is dangerous to turn your back on the truth. When you do that, a vacuum is created and nature abhors a vacuum. According to the Bible, what moves in when truth is expelled is a lie! **Romans 1:25** says,

> *Who changed the truth of God into a lie, and worshipped and served the creature more than the Creator, who is blessed for ever. Amen.*

When God's truth is rejected it is replaced by a lie. Probably the best example of this is the theory of evolution! Evolution has been "politically correct" for years. It is taught as fact and yet it is not supported by fact. Indeed Darwin's theory of evolution is a myth...a lie.

- **Myths are designed to deceive**

   For we have not followed cunningly devised fables. when we made known unto you the power and coming of our Lord Jesus Christ, but were eyewitnesses of his majesty. **2 Peter 1: 16**

A *"cunningly devised fable"* is one that is created to be acceptable. It is often introduced slowly and becomes increasingly popular. Now, I am not against fun. I still like to watch Bugs Bunny from time to time. But there is a difference between Bugs Bunny and Disney's *Lion King*. This animated Disney production teaches occult philosophy instead of biblical truth! It is a cunningly devised fable. In fact, in *The Green Egg*, a widely circulated occult magazine, it says *Lion King* "is without a doubt the most Pagan-positive movie ever to come out of Disney... "[4]

You must remember that **nearly all mythology is rooted in pagan religion and worship** and today there is a revival of pagan religion and worship. People are really believing in and worshipping Mother Nature. They communicate with Trolls (we know them as demons). They seek to contact nature spirits, fairies, nymphs, etc. There are those who really worship Diana/Artemis just as they did back in the Apostle Paul's time (Acts 19:24 & ff).

PART 2

What should be our response to myths?

- **Myths are to be ignored**

  > *I Timothy 1:4 Neither give heed to fables and endless genealogies, which minister questions, rather than godly edifying which is in faith so do.*

  > *Titus 1:14 Not giving heed to Jewish fables and commandments of men, that turn from the truth.*

In both verses we are told not to heed fables, myths. The "heed" means, **to hold in the mind; pay attention to or have regard for**. In other words, reject the myth. But that is not all. We are rather to PROMOTE THE TRUTH. This will lead to building up others.

Satan has cleverly disguised himself as an angel of light **(2 Corinthians. 11:14-15)**. I fear that many Christians are being bewitched by mythology and they don't even realize it. Remember the definition of mythology. Mythology is rooted in the teachings of pagan religions. People are being bewitched by mythology. Slowly but surely they are receiving and believing the occult doctrines that myths promote. **Colossians 2:8** warns,

> *Beware lest any man spoil you through philosophy and vain deceit, after the tradition of men, after the rudiments of the world, and not after Christ.*

Here are some examples of mythology being used

to bewitch Americans.

Cartoons & Animated Movies

Disney is one of the biggest offenders in this category. **The Little Mermaid** is a prime example of bringing pagan religion into American homes. The Little Mermaid's father is King Triton.

Poseidon, or Neptune   King Triton, Son of Poseidon

According to ancient pagan Greek religion Triton was the son of Poseidon and Amphitrite. Triton was the primitive pagan god who Zeus made responsible for seeing that the waters withdrew after the flood. He was half-man, half-fish and lived with his father in the depths of the sea. Triton supposedly could quiet the waves or stir the sea into a fury. He rode the waves on a chariot drawn by steeds

PART 2

whose hooves were the claws of crayfish. The pagan Greeks attributed the gift of prophecy to Triton. It is likely that the origin of the pagan god Triton goes back to Dagon, the pagan god of the Philistines mentioned in the Bible.[5]

Another example is the Disney production *Lion King.* This production is filled with New Age occult teachings. Let me give you the full quote from a leading occult magazine. I gave you a portion of the quote earlier in the book. Witch, Morning Glory Zell says that *Lion King*,

"is without a doubt the most Paganpositive movie ever to come out from

Disney, and it is now out there alongside of *Fern Gully and Captain Planet* teaching kids about why Mother Nature deserves our reverence and protection."[6]

I will not take the time to point out all the occult teachings in the movie Lion King. Suffice it to say that Rafiki the baboon is a shaman, a witch-doctor. "The accouterments of shamanic ritualism is graphically portrayed in the dedication of baby Simba to the spirits of the earth."[7]

Just a few words about Disney's *Pocahontas*. **First**, the story is revisionist. It does not portray history with any accuracy and though it may not have been intended to, children accept the cartoon version as historical fact. I know that is true, because I have asked them and get the Disney account not the historical account. **Second**, it promotes pantheism. The song, *Colors of The Wind* says, "Every rock and tree and creature has life, has spirit." **Third**, reincarnation is heavily advocated as well. Pocahontas sings, "The rainstorm and the river are my brothers, the heron and the otter are my friends, and we are all connected to each other in a circle, in a hoop, that never ends."

In reality, Matoaka, better known by her nick name Pocahontas, meaning "playful one" professed faith in Jesus Christ. She took the English name Rebecca, converted to Christianity and married John Rolfe in 1614 and gave birth to their son Thomas. The marriage brought about a much needed eight-year

PART 2

peace with the Algonquain Indians.

There are many more examples of mythology promoting the occult. But now, I want to move on to games that promote the occult.

Bewitched By Dungeons & Dragons

"Pass me the **Kleenex**, I dropped some **Jello** on my shirt." Perhaps you are wondering what that has to do with the history of Dungeons and Dragons. Let me explain. Kleenex is the brand name that introduced Americans to facial tissues. There are many more brands now...Puffs, Scotties, etc. and yet people still say, "pass the Kleenex, please." Then there is Jello, which is a brand name of gelatin. There are other brand names of gelatin as well, but when people want you to pass the dessert made of gelatin, they say, "pass the Jello." Dungeons and Dragons (also called D&D) fits into the same category. There are literally hundreds of Fantasy Role Playing (FRP) games, but because Dungeons and Dragons was the first, people often call any FRP game Dungeons and Dragons.

Here is a brief explanation of the game. The Dungeon Master (DM), who is the leader of the game, orchestrates the game. Each player assumes the identity of the character he creates by a roll of the dice. The object of the game is to maneuver your character, settings filled with dangerous monsters, enemy warriors and unforeseen traps and capture the treasure. If you are to survive you must equip yourself with a variety of weapons like daggers, lances, swords, axes, etc. But that's not all. You need special help, too. That comes from magic spells, talismen, magical weapons and divine help from the pagan gods and goddesses you must be devoted to. Each player can play the game as long as his character stays alive. Games can last from several hours to a year or more. The longer the game is played the more the player begins to identify with his or her character. This can cause problems. One D&D authority said, "The stuff that makes me nervous is over-identification with characters. I've seen people have fits, yell for fifteen minutes, hurl dice at a grand piano when their character dies." In fact, I know it gets worse than that. Occult specialist, Jack Roper, has shown me the case where a young man took his own life because his Dungeon Master informed him that his character had been killed. Folks, there is a problem here! There is more to Fantasy Role Playing Games than meets the eye. There are some dark facts about fantasy role playing games that you need to know!

THE ELEMENTS OF FANTASY ROLE PLAYING GAMES

I have spent more than one hundred hours researching Dungeons and Dragons and the FRP game spectrum and I have discovered seven strong elements within these games –

IDOL WORSHIP & MYTHOLOGY

PART 2

MAGIC, OCCULT & DEMONOLOGY
VIOLENCE, TORTURE & DEATH
SENSUALITY, LUST & IMMORALITY
MEDIEVAL TIMES
THE PREHISTORIC REALM
SCIENCE FICTION

MYTHOLOGY & IDOL WORSHIP

I want to repeat **2 Timothy 4:3-4**

> *For the time will come when they will not endure sound doctrine; but after their own lusts shall they heap to themselves teachers, having itching ears; And they shall turn away their ears from the truth, and shall be turned unto fables (myths or fantasies).*

I will also add to that **1 Corinthians 10:14:**

> *Wherefore, my dearly beloved, flee from idolatry.*

Pagan worship and bloody sacrifices play a part in most FRP games, even human sacrifice. Consider this information from a D&D magazine...

> Influence with the gods, as with any earthly authority, can be gained by bribes and services. The more a character does for his god, the more faithful he is and the more his god may look after him and try to help him out to some degree.
>
> The more important a god is, the more

The Dark Side of Halloween

it takes to impress him and win his favor...sacrifices are simple and effective for currying favor with a ...Clues to what would be a good sacrifice for each god can be found in reading about them and their exploits.

Human sacrifices of several types are also popular with certain gods of a more evil persuasion...worshippers are not above kidnapping their victims, or at least buying slaves for the altar. Some gods are very finicky about human sacrifices, preferring babies, or maidens...

Some gods like to have the sacrifice bled to death...others prefer immolation, drowning, or even drawing... Tezcat takes human sacrifices slain by having hearts torn out while they are still living.[8]

Here are some additional quotes from FRP books.

• **TYAA** (winged goddess of evil birds): Only women are permitted in the highpriesthood and Tyaa demands the sacrifice of body parts from her most attractive worshippers.[9]

• **GRUUMSH** Greater god; The proper worship of Gruumsh requires blood in large quantities, preferably blood of humans...

• **ARIOCH** The Knight of the Swords; The god Arioch usually takes his magical or fighting abilities

PART 2

into the Prime Material Plane. He always disdains the use of armor in battle and fights with a sword ...Those beings who know the proper rituals may attempt to summon Arioch from his home dimension. Would be summoners who pledge themselves to him and <u>offer him human sacrifices</u> may request aid or advice from Arioch, and if it suits his mood and increases his power on the Prime Material Plane, he may grant their request. Arioch is arrogant and short tempered.

- **DRUAGA** (ruler of the devil world) is a character from Babylonian mythology. Druaga will very occasionally send a group of devils out to aid his worshippers, especially those that have recently sacrificed a virgin to their deity.

- **KALI** (black earth mother) is a character from Indian mythology. This goddess is destruction incarnate, the ruthless mother who can give life and then take it away. She <u>eats her own children</u> for sustenance...she is so awesome in her destructiveness that she is able to inspire fear in even the most gruesome demons and devils. Her worship requires <u>sacrifices of blood</u> and even an <u>occasional human sacrifice</u>. Her cult includes many assassins. Those sworn to defend her cult will often do so in a sort of berserk, suicidal manner, slaying all who oppose them until they themselves are slain.

Often when I address this issue, when it comes to the question and answer time someone will say,

The Dark Side of Halloween

these gods and goddesses are all make believe, so what are you worrying about. The reality is that many of these gods and goddesses are and were actually worshipped and those who worshipped them actually performed the diabolical sacrifices required by these pagan deities. Their response is often "Oh sure!" Give me an example. That's just what I intend to do. The following came out of the Dungeons & Dragons publication *Deities & Demigods* –

- **TLALOC** (rain god): With his great tusks and goggle eyes, Tlalock's appearance is quite impressive. He wears all black but for a garland of white feathers. At each full moon, a priest of Tlaloc sacrifices a child or baby to Tlaloc. Once a year, there is a great festival held in his honor. Numerous babies are bought or taken from the populace. These babies are sacrificed to Tlaloc, after which the priests cook and eat them. If the babies cry during the sacrifice, this is taken as a good sign that rain will be abundant during the coming year. If the proper rituals and sacrifices have been followed to the letter, Tlaloc will usually grant his worshipers the rain they need. However, if he thinks his requirements have not been met, the people will be punished. Tlaloc has four pitchers of water: one filled with good water to make crops grow properly, one filled with water that contains spider's eggs and webs and causes blight, one filled with water that turns to frost, and one with water that rots all fruit.[10]

PART 2

- Where do the D&D people get their information? They get it from occult books and research about the occult. I am sure you will agree when you read what the **Larousse Encyclopedia of Mythology** has to say about **Tlaloc**.

  > Tlaloc (pulp of the earth) was the god of mountains, rain and springs. He belonged at first to the Otomi [tribe]. Like the foregoing he is painted black, but wears a garland of white feathers topped with a green plume. Among his attributes occurs the mask of a two-headed snake.
  >
  > Tlaloc lived on the mountain tops, and his dwelling Tlalocan was abundantly provided with food. There lived the goddess of cereals, and especially maize.
  >
  > Tlaloc owned four pitchers of water which he used for watering the earth. The water of the first was good, and helped the growth of maize and fruits; the water of the second produced spiders' webs and caused blight among the cereals; that of the third turned to frost, and that of the fourth destroyed all fruits.
  >
  > The cult of Tlaloc was the most horrible of all. Numerous children and babies at the breast were sacrificed to him. For the festival in his honour the priests started out to look for a large number

of babies which they bought from their mothers... After killing them, they cooked and ate them...If the children

cried and shed plenty of tears the spectators rejoiced, saying rain was coming.[11]

If you are ever in Mexico City, go to the Mexico museum. As you approach the front door of the Museum, there is a huge statue of Tlaloc. It is said that there is a revival of Tlaloc worship in parts of Mexico today. It does not take a rocket scientist to

PART 2

see where the writers of the D&D material got their information. My point is simply this. A great deal of the information included in FRP games comes from actual occult sources.

Now, I know there are still some people reading this who are saying, **It's only a game!** I have heard that statement echoed often enough by parents and teenagers! But, that is just not true! In fact, I want to go on record as sounding a warning **-BEWARE OF FANTASY ROLE PLAYING GAMES** (FRP). I have good reasons for saying that. Here's why. In more than a decade of counseling young people who have been drawn into occult groups and practices, I find that FRP games are a common denominator in increasing their appetite for the "power" and adventure the occult purports to offer. Allow me to submit a frightening illustration of how one teenager was drawn into the occult through *Dungeons and Dragons*. Matthew told me, "in Dungeons & Dragons if you are getting attacked by anything or if some situation is against you, you can use your magical power to face the situation and get your way out of it."

He went on to say that he and his friend wanted that kind of power, the kind of power that the characters in the games had. They believed that the magical powers used by the characters in the "games" were real and were available, so they began to delve deeper into the occult. Matthew reasoned, "if we have these magical, special types of power that are real, when we face the

The Dark Side of Halloween

adversities of life we will be able to take care of business. And we thought it would make us more popular... "

Matthew did pursue occult powers and the results were frightening! He began doing magic rituals and offering blood sacrifices, just like the characters in the FRP games he had played. Here is his account in his own words ...

> We built one outpost in the woods for seasonal ceremonies. We would hold our mass-type worship services there. We also had a second sight that we used for quick sanctuary type ceremonies. We used an old abandoned bridge that went across the bike trail in the woods. We painted it all up with different symbols. We'd hang out there and smoke pot and do the basic rituals. Rituals were really easy to find in books from the public library or even in the school libraries. We were trying desperately to gain power through all this. We started doing (blood) sacrifices. We started off with a bird. We actually thought if we have blood in the sacrifices, it will honor the demon more and the demon will be more pleased and he will work on our behalf to a greater extent. When that did not work, we started to sacrifice bigger animals and do more rituals. We thought if we follow these sacrifices we

PART 2

> will have this kind of power. But the bad thing that happens is, when you are sitting there and you are trying to do all these rituals, there was that power there but it took our mind frame to different level. When you are killing things and seeing which way their entrails move after they are dead, and you are actually getting joy from this, your mind has taken a dark slide into sickness. Couple that with the fact that we were doing a lot of drugs, life and your own life means very little to you.

I remind you again how Matthew got started. He said:

> In Dungeons & Dragons if you are getting attacked by anything or if some situation is against you, you can use your magical power to face the situation and get your way out of it...If we have these magical, special types of power that are real, when we face the adversities of life we will be able to take care of business. And we thought it would make us more popular...

Matthew was drawn into the occult through a Fantasy Role Playing Game called *Dungeons and Dragons*. His is not an isolated incident. Similar scenarios are being played out all over this and other countries. I well remember when I began researching this topic, coming across these words. by an Australian. He had been a high priest in a grotto that practiced black magick. He told *The Sunday Mail*, "I've been involved in the occult for years, and the packaging of these fantasy games is the greatest introduction to witchcraft and demonology I've ever seen."[12]

Listen, many who play FRP games are drawn into the occult. In fact, **I believe that FRP games recruit many youth for occultists**. Occultists look for young people who are really into FRP games because they know their minds are conditioned to occult ideals and practices. They want the occult powers being used in their "games" to be used in their daily lives. I hope you can see why you need to **BEWARE OF FANTASY ROLE PLAYING GAMES.** They are an open door to the fearful, diabolical world of the occult. If you have any FRP materials (books, magazines, manuals, video games, board games, cards, etc.) you should do the same thing they did with occult material in **Acts 19:19-20** –

> *"Many of them also which used curious arts brought their books together, and burned them before all men: and they counted the price of them, and found it fifty thousand pieces of silver. So mightily grew the word of God and prevailed."*

There are so many more games that promote the occult that it is impossible to cover them all. But, I would like to look at one more.

PART 2

Magic Cards

The technical name for this card game is *Magic: The Gathering*™. So what is the basis of Magic Cards? Let me quote from the *Washington Post*.

> "Unlike Dungeons and Dragons, which became an infamous tool for occultists, Magic has not developed an outside mythology. 'This draws on the milieu, the fantasy of Dungeons and Dragons' says Richard Garfield, the creative impetus behind Magic ... "[13]

Magic cards are based on the occult mythology of Dungeons and Dragons.

Georgia Pabst of the *Milwaukee Journal Sentinel* writes,

> "Magic: The Gathering takes place in the mystical multiverse of Dominia where players become mighty wizards and, armed with beautifully illustrated cards of various creatures, artifacts and lands, cast spells and enchantment aimed at killing off the opponent."[14]

The Dark Side of Halloween

Georgia, in the above concise statement, hits the nail on the head. Every player is a wizard or sorcerer and the goal is to build up enough magic energy to kill your opponent. Here's how it works according to the instruction book that comes with the cards –

> "There are two basic types of cards: spells and lands. Lands are easy to spot; they say 'land' in between the picture and the text box. Lands are the most common kind of card in Magic, since they usually provide the mana, or magical energy, for all your spells. You can lay out one land per turn, and you may use the land for mana as soon as it is in play."[15]

Now, how do you kill your opponent? Aimee Miller of the Washington Post wrote,

> "The rules of the game are simple: Each player starts with 20 'lifepoints.'

PART 2

> You gain lifepoints by casting beneficial spells from land cards. You lose lifepoints when attacked by nasty creatures and charms. If you run out of lifepoints, you're exiled, which is a polite way of saying your're dead. Players stay alive by annihilating their opponents first."[16]

She goes on to say,

> "Want to crush your opponent in under five minutes? Stack the deck with deadly and destructive black and red Magic cards."[17]

That brings me to the Mana (magical energy) Chart explaining the different kinds of Magic and how they can be used.

Black Magic is identified as the magic of death. Let me share with you two quotes from the book, *Mastering Magic Cards*.

> "The magic of death is often a double-edged sword, however, malevolent to its wielder as well as its victim. Few people summon the awesome might of the Lord of the Pit without being ready to sacrifice their very worldly existence to wild its incredible power... "[18]

The second quote –

> "A black necromancer wields the sacrifice, particularly the Dark Ritual Cards."[19]

The Dark Side of Halloween

Blue Magic is mental in nature and taps "the elemental forces of air and water." Friends, lest you think this is harmless let me tell you that occultists believe in and seek to tap into the power of what they call Sylphs (elemental spirits of the air). They believe that Lucifer empowers air spirits. That is interesting in light of **Ephesians 2:2**

> *Wherein in time past ye walked according to the course of this world, according to the prince of the power of the air, the spirit that now worketh in the children of disobedience:*

The truth is, the elemental spirits that occultists claim to communicate with, whether they be air, water, earth or fire spirits are demons from Satan's diabolical horde. I have personally interviewed a real witch who says she invokes earth spirits known as trolls (really demons) to assist her in her rituals. (order -*The Truth About Trolls* for more information). Magic cards is conditioning children to be receptive to paganism.

Green Magic draws energy from the forest and has vast destructive capabilities. Green or Ecological magic is in fact one of the most popular forms of witchcraft today.

Red Magic is the destructive magic of earth, fire, chaos and war. Chaotic magic is practiced by many today. There are Internet sites devoted solely to this diabolical form of magic.

White Magic is used for protection, healing

PART 2

injuries and chivalrous war. Wiccans claim to practice only this "good" kind of magic. I know that is not true. You have read earlier in this book some of curses that "good witches" have spit out against Christians. And let me remind you that occult magic in any form is derived from Satan and his diabolical horde.

Now, I can almost hear the protests again. It's only a game! But, many of those who play Magic cards identify mentally with the Sorcerer they choose to play. Consider this quote –

> "Part of the game's appeal comes from 'the ability to develop a character - you get to be somebody else.' says Garfield. In Magic the deck you put together reflects your character-your persona."[20]

Magic cards and all the clones, SPELLFIRE™, GUARDIANS™, HIGHLANDER™, WYVERN™, VAMPIRE™, BloodWars™, SHADOWFIST™, HYBORIAN GATES, RAGE COMBAT, TOWERS IN TIME™, On the Edge/ARCANA, EVERWAY™, etc. are all steeped in occult teachings!

It is hard to know where to stop. I have not even exposed the occult nature of the popular *Goosebumps* book series and the, so called, "Christian" horror series *Spine Chillers*. They are laced with occult material. And do you know what readers graduate to? They move up to Steven King and Anne Rice books that are worse. Logos carries a published report dealing with this topic.

It is not possible for me to deal with all the trash that is out there. It is difficult for me not to write a dozen more pages on the occult and violent themes in video games, not to mention TV. But what I have decided to do is to write one last chapter that will give you biblical guidelines for determining what is acceptable and what is not.

The Yardstick for Determining Acceptability

There is a battle going on for the minds of our children and grandchildren. In fact, Satan and his diabolical hordes want to corrupt the minds of adults as well! One of the problems is that Satan is getting the upper hand because Christians are oblivious to the tactics the adversary is using to pollute the minds of men, women, boys and girls. While many Christian adults would catch blatant demonic doctrines, the truth is, Satan seldom mounts a direct assault on believers or their children. Rather, he, through his human helpers uses subtle, clandestine and deceptive methods to advance his evil doctrines and corrupt values. Let's look at two classic Bible passages that point out how our subtle adversary often operates.

Matthew 7:15 calls them <u>wolves in sheep's clothing</u>. The next passage is **2 Corinthians 11:13-15.** In this passage Satan's messengers are called *"deceitful workers"* who pretend to be apostles of Christ but are not. The passage goes on to say that *"Satan himself is transformed into an angel of light"* and *"his ministers"* also claim to be

PART 2

"the ministers of righteousness."

So, how can we protect ourselves and our children? The Bible tells us that whatever we do is to glorify God. **1 Corinthians 10:31** says, *Whether therefore ye eat, or drink, or whatsoever ye do, do all to the glory of God.* What does that mean? Simply stated, a Christian should **do only those things that our Lord would approve of**. Since God is concerned with the things that we eat and drink, I believe that he is also concerned with the books we read, the TV programs we watch, the music we listen to, the games we play, etc.

So how can we determine whether something is good or evil, right or wrong. How can we practice the **Romans 12:9** which says, *"... Abhor that which is evil; cleave to that which is good."* Is there a yardstick that we can use to make this determination?

The answer is **YES!** The **Holy Bible** is the "yardstick" we are to use to determine whether something is acceptable or unacceptable (right or wrong). The Bible tells us what's right, what's hot right, how to get right and how to stay right. Look at **2 Timothy 3:16** *All scripture is given by inspiration of God, and is profitable for doctrine* (what's right), *for reproof* (what's not right), *for correction* (how to get right), *for instruction in righteousness* (how to stay right).

Obviously, it is impossible for our Logos staff to review every book, TV program, game, toy, video game, video, music CD, etc. that comes on the market and then report to you whether they glorify· God. However, we do try to review the most popular ones. But there is something that we can do that will enable you to discern whether these things measure up to the **Biblical Yardstick.** Below are some key Biblical guidelines that will assist you in making Christ-honoring choices when it comes to the books that you read, music you listen to, TV/videos you watch, etc.

BIBLICAL GUIDELINES FOR DETERMINING ACCEPTABILITY

What belief system is being promoted?

There are an increasing number of books, TV/video programs, etc. that are promoting belief systems (religions) other than Christian. The apostle Paul wrote to young Timothy and warned him,

> Now the Spirit speaketh expressly, that in the latter times some shall depart from the faith, giving heed to seducing spirits, and doctrines of devils; **1 Timothy 4:1**.

Some examples that promote non-Christian belief systems are:
1) **Lion King** books, games, CD's, tapes and toys. A shaman (witch doctor), Rafiki, dedicates young Simba to the spirits of the earth.
2) **Pocahontas** books, videos and tapes teaches Animism.
3) **Star Trek** promotes Eastern New Age doctrines
4) **Hercules & Xena** television programs are based on Roman and Greek pagan religion.

What philosophy or system of values does the game promote?

> **Colossians 2:8** *Beware lest any man spoil you through philosophy and vain deceit, after the tradition of men, after the rudiments of the world, and not after Christ.*

The Dark Side of Halloween

A person derives his or her philosophy from one of the two primary sources of wisdom. **James 3:15-17** reveals the origin of these two sources of wisdom.

> *This <u>wisdom</u> descendeth <u>not from above</u>, but is earthly, sensual, devilish. For where envying and strife is, there is confusion and every evil work. But the <u>wisdom that is from above</u> is first pure, then peaceable, gentle, and easy to be entreated, full of mercy and good fruits, without partiality, and without hypocrisy.*

The wisdom from above is God's wisdom which leads to purity, peace, kindness and more. The wisdom that is not from above is Satan's wisdom that is worldly (earthly), appeals to our old nature (sensual) and is demonic (devilish).

The values promoted in books, games, etc. should <u>be consistent with God's wisdom and values as revealed in the Bible</u>. Honesty, diligence, truthfulness, kindness, self-control, sexual morality etc. are part of the Judea-Christian Ethic, that is, Old Testament—New Testament values (Biblical Values). When values are promoted based on Satan's wisdom, things like dishonesty, laziness, lying, violence, rebellion, immodesty, sexual immorality, the game must be rejected. **Romans 12:2** urges us –

> *And be not conformed to this world:*

PART 2

but be ye transformed by the renewing of your mind, that ye may prove what is that good, and acceptable, and perfect, will of God.

Listed below are just a few of **the godless philosophies of this world**. Keep your eyes open for them. Abhor that which is evil; cleave to that which is good. **Romans 12:9**

Unbiblical Philosophy	Basic Teaching	Biblical Perspective
Humanism (Characterized by love of self)	The belief that man is the highest authority. What is best for me is best.	*Isaiah 55:8-9 For my thoughts are not your thoughts, neither are your ways my ways, saith the LORD. 9 For as the heavens are higher than the earth, so are my ways higher than your ways, and my thoughts than your thoughts.*
Materialism (Characterized by the love of money)	The belief that physical wellbeing and worldly possessions constitute the greatest good and highest value in life	*1 Timothy 6:10 For the love of money is the root of all evil: which while some coveted after, they have erred from the faith, and pierced themselves through with many sorrows.*

The Dark Side of Halloween

Hedonism (Characterized by the love of pleasure)	The belief that the pursuit of or devotion to pleasure, especially to the pleasures of the senses is most important. In short, "if it feels good do it!"	**2 Timothy 3:4-5** *... lovers of pleasures more than lovers of God; **5** ... from such turn away.*
Relativism (Characterized by the belief that there are no absolutes)	The belief that truth and moral values are not absolute but are relative to the persons or groups holding them.	**Ecclesiastes 12:13** *Let us hear the conclusion of the whole matter: Fear God, and keep his commandments: for this is the whole duty of man.*
Pragmatism (Characterized by the belief, if it works use it)	The belief that the end justifies the means.	**Proverbs 14:12** *There is a way which seemeth right unto a man, but the end thereof are the ways of death.*
Machiavellianism (Characterized by use of deceit and lying to accomplish goals)	The belief that craft and deceit are justified in pursuing and maintaining power.	**Colossians 3:9** *Lie not one to another, seeing that ye have put off the old man with his deeds;* **2 Timothy 3:13** *But evil men and seducers shall wax worse and worse, deceiving, and being deceived.*

PART 2

| Evolutionism (Characterized by belief that man is only a high functioning animal) | The belief that man evolved and is evolving from a simple form of life to a more complex form over millions of years. | *Genesis 1:1 In the beginning God created the heaven and the earth.* |

Books and reading material, music, videos, games, in fact everything that does not promote philosophies and values that are consistent with the Bible should be rejected. Why, because everything we do is to glorify God -*Whether therefore ye eat, or drink, or whatsoever ye do, do all to the glory of God.* **1 Corinthians 10:31**

Is there a "power" portrayed and if so, what is the source or origin of it?

The Lord God of Heaven is omnipotent (all powerful). In fact, we are told *"...that power belongeth unto God."* **Psalms 62:11**. Further, we are told to *"...sing and praise."* God's power **Psalms 21:13**. But there is a BIG PROBLEM when power is derived from a source other than from the Lord God Almighty. Many books, games, toys, etc. feature occult pantheistic power sources at work. They energize the characters. They control circumstances. This is an abomination to the Lord God of Heaven. While Satan is a powerful adversary, God is greater! We must not honor the power of our adversary the devil. That brings me to the next point...

The Dark Side of Halloween

Where are the person's imagination and thoughts being directed?

Imagination can be a powerful force for good or evil. When I was a young child I used to imagine that I was a fireman. My dad would let me put on his fireman's helmet and I would run around the house putting out fires and rescuing my teddy bear, my sister and my dog from impending danger. This was a wholesome use of my imagination and it did influence me in later years. When I grew up I served as a fireman on several volunteer fire departments and one paid department.

Another illustration of the proper use of the imagination took place at my grandparent's home. I would regularly go over to visit them. One of my favorite toys was called a View Master. My grandad had a number of View Master picture disks of the National Parks and other sights in the western United States. Those pictures stimulated within my mind the desire to visit those places one day and in fact, I have traveled to every one of those destinations and more.

But, let me also sound a **WARNING** loud and clear. If the things you let into your mind are unwholesome your thoughts will be directed in that way. Here is an example for your consideration. Dungeons & Dragons (and other fantasy role playing games) are filled with the occult, the occult power of magic, violence, and more. Dungeons &

PART 2

Dragons drew Matthew into the world of the occult. He reasoned -"in D&D if you are getting attacked by anything if something is against you, you can use your magical powers to face the situation and get your way out of it." He went on to say that D&D gave him the desire for real magical powers. He said, "If we have these magical types of power that are real, when we face the adversities of life we will be able to take care of business." Matthew and his friend got involved in the real occult, including animal sacrifice. Why? Because he did not guard his mind.

The Bible says, **Proverbs 4:23**

> *Keep thy heart with all diligence; for out of it are the issues of life. Further, vain imaginations will lead to a darkened heart.*

Romans 1 :21

> *Because that, when they knew God, they glorified him not as God, neither were thankful; but became vain in their imaginations. and their foolish heart was darkened ..*

2 Corinthians 10:4-5

> *(For the weapons of our warfare are not carnal, but mighty through God to the pulling down of strong holds;) Casting down imaginations, and every high thing that exalteth itself against the knowledge of God, and bringing*

into captivity every thought to the obedience of Christ;

Does it magnify fear, glorify evil, promote violence, gore or death?

FEAR

Goosebumps and Fear Street books are the best selling books to middle school and junior high young people today. These are horror books. They engender fear in the hearts of many young readers.

The Bible warns us that this is not good because fear brings mental torment (1 John 4:18) In fact, many of those who read such things are tormented by nightmares, feelings of insecurity, and anxiety, just to mention a few.

The Scriptures tell us that we are to focus our thoughts on things that are true, noble, right, pure, lovely, and amiable **(Philippians 4:8)**. When these things are the focus of our thoughts we are told - And the peace of God, which passeth all understanding, shall keep your hearts and minds through Christ Jesus. **Philippians 4:7** The truth is, we need to steer away from books, games, videos/TV that cause our minds to fear because fear leads to an unsound mind. The Bible says, *For God hath not given us the spirit of fear; but of power, and of love, and of a sound mind.* **2 Timothy 1 :7**

PART 2

I would remind you that our thoughts are to be focused on things that please God. **Colossians 3:2** tells us, *Set your affection on things above, not on things on the earth*. Verse 15 of the same chapter says, *"And let the peace of God rule in your hearts..."* **Isaiah 26:3** adds this—*Thou wilt keep him in perfect peace, whose mind is stayed on thee: because he trusteth in thee.*

Don't expose your minds to the horror genera that is so prevalent today. These things do not glorify God. One more thing Dr. Grace Ketterman, M.D. warns –

> "a tragic by-product of fear in the lives of children as early as pre-adolescence is the interest and involvement in supernatural occult phenomena."[21]

EVIL & VIOLENCE

Our day to day world abounds in evil and violence. We should not magnify evil and violence by exposing ourselves to it needlessly. When we do, we become callused and may even develop an appetite for it. Several Bible passages that relate to this are -

Romans 12:9b *Abhor that which is evil; cleave to that which is good.*

Psalms 97:10a *Ye that love the LORD, hate evil:*

Psalms 11:5 *The LORD trieth the righteous: but the wicked and him that loveth violence his soul hateth.*

Are occult, New Age or other pagan practices included?

(sorcery, magic, fortune-telling, necromancy, witches., psychic powers, "the force," aliens, transformation, etc.)

When God says something is wrong, it is wrong regardless of what form it is in. The occult is an abomination to the Lord regardless of whether it is in comic form, video form, book form, toy form, etc. Occult practices are an abomination to the Lord. The power behind the occult is demonic (see Acts 16:16-18). God does not want us involved in the occult in any way -

Deuteronomy 18:10-13

> *There shall not be found among you any one that maketh his son or his daughter to pass through the fire, or that useth divination, or an observer of times, or an enchanter, or a witch, Or a charmer, or a consulter with familiar spirits, or a wizard, or a necromancer. For all that do these things are an abomination unto the LORD: and because of these abominations the LORD thy God doth drive them out from before thee. Thou shalt be perfect with the LORD thy God.*

It is important to note the Biblical evaluation of those involved in the occult is found in **Acts 13:10:**

> *0 full of all subtlety and all mischief,*

> thou child of the devil, thou enemy of all righteousness, wilt thou not cease to pervert the right ways of the Lord?

We clearly see what we are to do with materials related to the occult.

Acts 19:19

> Many of them also which used curious arts brought their books together, and burned them before all men: and they counted the price of them, and found it fifty thousand pieces of silver.

Is it sensual or vulgar?'.

Psalms 101:3 *I will set no wicked thing before mine eyes: I hate the work of them that turn aside; it shall not cleave to me.*

Job 31:1 *I made a covenant with mine eyes; why then should I think upon a maid?*

The words *"think upon"* means to separate mentally. The writer is implying that he would not look sensually upon a woman. Materials that promote sensual or vulgar themes should be avoided.

The Dark Side of Halloween

- **THE RIGHT TYPE OF BOOKS, GAMES, MUSIC, VIDEOS & TOYS TO BUY**
- **THOSE THAT PROMOTE BIBLICAL VALUES & CHARACTER**
- **THOSE THAT DEVELOP SKILLS**
- **THOSE THAT ARE EDUCATIONAL YET BIBLICAL**
- **THOSE THAT STIMULATE WHOLESOME IMAGINATION & CREATIVITY**

These guidelines give you a biblical yardstick by which to measure television programs, videos, games, books, activities, etc. If they do not measure up, then they should be rejected.

> *Whatsoever ye do, do all to the glory of God.* 1 Corinthians 10:31

> *And have no fellowship with the unfruitful works of darkness, but rather reprove them.* Ephesians 5:11

DON'T PLAY RUSSIAN ROULETTE WITH YOUR SOUL!

RUSSIAN ROULETTE is a gambling game. The stakes are high, you might say, you bet your life! As I understand it Russian Roulette got its name from a practice the KGB used to elicit information from those they interrogated. Here's how it worked. A bullet was placed into one of the chambers of the revolver. Then the KGB agent would ask the prisoner for information. If he did not get a satisfactory answer, the cylinder was closed and then spun, the hammer cocked, the gun

PART 2

placed to the head of the prisoner and the trigger pulled. If the hammer came down on an empty chamber, the pris-oner lived, at least long enough to be asked another question. If the hammer came down on the bullet in the chamber, the prisoner died. Many died at the hands of the KGB playing Russian Roulette.

Unfortunately, from time to time, we read about people who willingly play this deadly game. Perhaps it is played more often than we would like to think, because the people we read about are those who bet their life and lost. I remember the story of an actor who played Russian Roulette and lost. It was in the summer of 1985. Between filming movie scenes, macho-man actor John Eric Hexum was just fooling around. He placed a blank shell in the revolver he was using in the movie. No doubt he thought that blanks were harm-less. He spun the cylinder, placed it to his temple, pulled the trigger and blasted the wadding of the blank into his temple. He played Russian Roulette and lost. It cost him his life!

By now, perhaps you are wondering, "What is the point?" Let me make my point clear. While it is highly unlikely that anyone reading this article has ever or will ever be foolish enough to play Russian Roulette with a revolver, I believe there are many who, this very moment, are playing RUSSIAN ROULETTE WITH THEIR SOULS!

What does it mean to play Russian Roulette with your soul?

When I refer to "playing Russian Roulette with your soul" I am referring to those who gamble on their eternal destiny by either being ignorant of, or ignoring what the Bible says about how to be saved from your sins and go to Heaven. The Bible says you can know for sure that you have eternal life (are going to Heaven when you die). **1 John 5:13** says,

> *These things have I written unto you that believe on the name of the Son of God; that ye may know that ye have eter-nal life, and that ye may believe on the name of the Son of God.*

As you can see from **1 John 5:13**, belief on the Son of God, Jesus Christ is the key to knowing where you are going when you die. Jesus himself said,

> *I am the way, the truth, and the life: no man cometh unto the Father, but by me.* **John 14:6**.

Peter the Apostle put it this way –

> *Neither is there salvation in any other: for there is none other name under heaven given among men, whereby we must be saved.* **Acts 4: 12**

I've shared this Gospel of Salvation with thousands of people over the past twenty-five years. Praise

PART 2

the Lord, hundreds have trusted Christ as their personal Savior. But, many that I have witnessed to are playing Russian Roulette with their souls. They are gambling that they won't go to Hell when they die. Over the years I have seen seven common ways people play Russian Roulette with their souls. I'm going to liken each one to a bullet placed into a gun.

Seven Common Ways People Play Russian Roulette With Their Souls

- **BULLET #1 - Believing Infant Baptism Will Get You To Heaven**

One of the counterfeit doctrines that Satan has used effectively to obscure Biblical Salvation is the false doctrine of infant baptism. This damnable doctrine has deceived millions of adults into believing that because they had water sprinkled on their heads in a church service when they i.yere babies, somehow this makes them fit for Heaven. That's a lie. There is not one single verse in the entire Bible that tells us that babies should be baptized. The truth is, only believers, those who have trusted in Christ, are commanded to be baptized. **(Acts 8:36-38)**

I'll never forget the first time I ran into this unbiblical doctrine. It was at a funeral. The person conducting the funeral waxed eloquent at the beginning of the service about this man's infant baptism. According to the comments, infant baptism somehow was supposed to make it possible for him to get into Heaven, provided enough candles were lit and enough masses were said. If the man in the casket believed what the speaker was saying, he had played Russian Roulette with his soul... and lost.

My friend, if you believe that your infant baptism saves you from your sins and makes you fit for Heaven, then you too are gambling with your soul and you will lose.

- **BULLET #2 - There Are Many Roads To Heaven**

It seems to me that this is one of the most popular fallacies being believed today. I have had many people tell me that this is what they believe. One incident that stands out in my mind is my interview with a witch. I had asked her if she knew Christ as her Savior. She responded by saying that it did not matter whether you believed in the Great Spirit, Buddha or Christ, etc. because these all were paths to God.

Popular or not, if you believe that there are many roads to God you are in for a shock the moment you die. You will find yourself in Hell and too late you will realize the truth of what the Bible says in **Matthew 7:13-14:**

> *Enter ye in at the strait (narrow) gate: for wide is the gate, and broad is the way, that leadeth to destruction, and*

PART 2

> *many there be which go in thereat: Because strait is the gate, and narrow is the way, which leadeth unto life, and few there be that find it.*

There are many on the road to destruction. That is a. broad road. But there is only one door to the narrow way that leads to eternal life and Jesus Christ is that door. **John 10:7-9**

> *Then said Jesus unto them again, Verily, verily, I say unto you, I am the door of the sheep. All that ever came before me are thieves and robbers: but the sheep did not hear them. I am the door: by me if any man enter in, he shall be saved, and shall go in and out, and find pasture.*

You are playing Russian Roulette with your soul if you buy the lie that there are many paths to God. There is just one path to God. That path is through Jesus Christ the Lord. Allow me to repeat **John 14:6** again –

> *Jesus saith unto him, I am the way, the truth, and the life: no man cometh unto the Father, but by me.*

- **BULLET #3 - Religious Service & Good Works Will Get You To Heaven**

During my first pastorate, I met an interesting old fellow. He was around 80 and he shared many interesting stories about Michigan history with me. I witnessed to him time and time again to no avail.

The Dark Side of Halloween

Each time he would relate to me how he had been a choir boy. That was the bullet in his gun. He was gambling that his good works as a choir boy would take him to Heaven. But they were worthless. **Ephesians 2:8-9** tells us,

> *For by grace are ye saved through faith; and that not of yourselves: it is the gift of God: Not of works, lest any man should boast.*

Titus 3:5 says,

> *Not by works of righteousness which we have done, but according to his mercy he saved us, by the washing of regeneration, and renewing of the Holy Ghost;*

John 3:16-18 makes it clear that only believing in Christ can save us from condemnation –

> *For God so loved the world, that he gave his only begotten Son, that whosoever believeth in him should not perish, but have everlasting life. For God sent not his Son into the world to condemn the world; but that the world through him might be saved. He that believeth on him is not condemned: but he that believeth not is condemned already, because he hath not believed in the name of the only begotten Son of God.*

The family called upon me to do the old

PART 2

gentleman's funeral. It was a hard one to do, because the man had gambled with his soul and lost!

What about you? Are you playing Russian Roulette with your soul?

- **BULLET #4 - Belief In God Will Get You To Heaven**

The grocery business sure has changed since I was a 4-year-old. My parents used to take me to the little grocery store when they went shopping. They would sit me on the counter and then pick up what they needed in that four-aisle store. If things weren't too busy, the butcher would come out from behind the meat counter and talk with me. As I got older I would ride my bike the three or four blocks to that store and pick up things mom needed. I would always go back and talk to the butcher. He was my friend. In my late teen years I tried to witness to him. His response was, "I believe in God. We're all working to get to the same place. If we do the best we can I think we'll all get there, Dave."

That was his answer. That was the end of the conversation. He did not want to talk about it anymore. He had loaded his gun with that lie and he was betting his eternal soul on it! May God yet open his eyes to the truth of the Scriptures!

Look at **James 2:19**

> *Thou believest that there is one God; thou doest well: the devils a/so*

believe, and tremble.

There is absolutely no saving merit in believing in God. The devil even does that much! You see, God is the one who laid out the plan of Salvation.

1 John 4:14 gives us a look at his plan.

> *And we have seen and do testify that the Father sent the Son to be the Saviour of the world.*

God has ordained that Salvation from our sins and Heaven comes only through his Son. If you really believed in God, you would do what he said.

1 John 2:23 issues a solemn warning

> *Whosoever denieth the Son, the same hath not the Father...*

If you think that believing in God is going to keep you out of Hell you are gambling on a losing proposition.

- **BULLET #5 -Phony Decisions For Chris,**

One nationally known pastor said that he thought 50% of the people in his congregation who claimed to be Christians were not. I don't know about that, but I do remember a man who had been a Sunday School teacher, a trustee and a deacon in a Baptist Church where I had been the assistant pastor. I knew the man. He was busy for the Lord. I would have never guessed that he was not really a Christian. I was surprised to learn that he had been playing Russian Roulette with his soul for almost

PART 2

20 years. He finally gave it up. He unloaded the gun and put his faith in Christ. He had made a counterfeit decision years earlier so he could marry a Christian girl. For years he was too proud to admit he was not really saved. Finally, after a major financial set back, he came to his senses and trusted Christ.

Listen friends,

> *Not every one that saith unto me, Lord, Lord, shall enter into the kingdom of heaven ...* **(Matthew 7:21)**.

You can use His name, you can pray, you can read the Bible, sing in the choir, teach a Sunday School class, but if you have never confessed that you are a sinner, repented of your sins and personally put your faith in Jesus Christ, you are not saved! You are playing Russian Roulette with your soul. I urge you to respond to **2 Corinthians 13:5**

> *Examine yourselves, whether ye be in the faith; prove your own selves. Know ye not your own selves, how that Jesus Christ is in you, except ye be reprobates?*

- **BULLET #6 -Following False Teachers & Faulty Philosophies**

Matthew 7:15 warns,

> *Beware of false prophets, which come to you in sheep's clothing, but inwardly they are ravening wolves.*

The Dark Side of Halloween

I interviewed a wolf in sheep's clothing. His name was Benjamin Creme. He claims to speak for the Christ (Lord Maitreya). In my interview I discovered he does not believe that all men are sinners. He says that the teachings of Christ are relative, not absolute, the sex act (in or outside of marriage) becomes divine if performed with sincerity of spirit, and he claims that Self-Realization, that is realizing that you are God, is the way to Heaven or Nirvana. Creme claims that God is an entity scalled Sanat Kumara, who came from Venus. We should worship him. **1 Timothy 4:1-2**

> *Now the Spirit speaketh expressly, that in the latter times some shall depart from the faith, giving heed to seducing spirits, and doctrines of devils; Speaking lies in hypocrisy; having their conscience seared with a hot iron;*

There are many false prophets, numerous false Christ's and bizarre doctrines that are as prevalent as manure in a stockyard. Read and heed the words of the Apostle Paul, **Galatians 1:6-9**

> *I marvel that ye are so soon removed from him that called you into the grace of Christ unto another gospel: Which is not another; but there be some that trouble you, and would pervert the gospel of Christ. But though we, or an angel from heaven, preach any other gospel unto you than that which we*

PART 2

> have preached unto you, let him be accursed. As we said before, so say I now again, If any man preach any other gospel unto you than that ye have received, let him be accursed.

Listen to the words of the Apostle John -**1 John 2:22**

> Who is a liar but he that denieth that Jesus is the Christ? He is antichrist, that denieth the Father and the Son.

If you have believed another Gospel than the Bible Gospel, if you have followed another Christ than the Bible Christ, if you are believing another doctrine than a Bible doctrine you are playing Russian Roulette with your soul!

- **BULLET #6 -Procrastination: Putting Off A Decision For Christ**

I was listening to Evangelist Fred Brown preach in Grand Rapids probably 15 years ago. He told us about an attractive teenager he had been witnessing to. He invited her to come to the evangelistic meetings and she came. It was obvious that she was under conviction, but she did not respond to the invitation. The evangelist met her at the back door and urged her to be saved, but she would not be persuaded. She said, "I've got too much living to do. Perhaps when I am older." He pleaded with her reminding her of **2 Corinthians. 6:2:**

The Dark Side of Halloween

> *Behold, now is the accepted time; behold, now is the day of salvation.*

She left without receiving Christ. Later that evening she was killed in a fiery car crash. Tragically, she had played Russian Roulette with her soul and lost.

In summary, I have shared with you **SEVEN COMMON WAYS THAT PEOPLE PLAY RUSSIAN ROULETTE WITH THEIR SOULS...**

1. They rely on infant baptism thinking it will get them to Heaven
2. They believe there are many paths to God
3. They trust in their religious activities & good works to get them to Heaven
4. They think belief in God is all that matters
5. They made a phony decision for Christ
6. They follow false teachers & faulty philosophies
7. They procrastinate: I'll trust Christ later

Are you Playing Russian Roulette With Your Soul? If so, STOP! Receive Jesus Christ as your Savior right now. The Bible says,

> *For whosoever shall call upon the name of the Lord shall be saved.* **Romans 10:13**

Why not call upon the Lord Jesus right now and ask him to Save you from the guilt, penalty and power of your sins.

Pray something like this -

PART 2

Dear Lord Jesus,

I confess that I am a sinner and need your forgiveness. I believe that you, Lord Jesus Christ, died for my sins and rose again from the dead. I now trust only in you, Christ, to save me from my sins and take me to Heaven. Come into my life, forgive my sins and save my soul. Thank you for hearing my prayer. AMEN

If you have made a decision to trust Christ as you Savior as a result of reading this article, drop me a note. See the address in the front of the book.

If you are a believer already, live your life to the glory of God each day. And, share Christ with as many people as you can, because after all, **2 Corinthians 5:20** tells us that *"we are ambassadors for Christ ... "*

May God richly bless you.

ENDNOTES—PART 1

1 Joy A. Sterling; *Moody Monthly- We Should Unmask Halloween*; October 1975; p 83
2 Linda Shepherd; *Moody Monthly, Getting a Handle On Halloween*; October 1993; p. 58
3 *Encyclopedia Britannica - 11th Edition*; Volume 12; p.858
4 Ralph Linton; *Halloween Through the Centuries*
5 *World Book Encyclopedia* - 1991 Edition; p. 24, 25
6 Stuart Piggott; *The Druids*; Thames & Hudson, 1993; p.109-110
7 Gerhard Herm; *The Celts*
8 *Man, Myth and Magic*; edited by Richard Cavendish; v. 6, p. 720
9 George William Douglas; *The American Book of Days*© 1970; pp.569 & 571
10 Alexander Hislop; *The Two Babylons*; Loizeaux Brothers, Neptune New Jersey; p.103
11 Ibid.; p 232
12 Ibid.;
13 Doreen Valiente; *An ABC of Witchcraft Past & Present*©1973; pp. 164-165
14 Margot Adler; *Drawing Down The Moon*; Beacon Press© 1986
15 Sharon Graham; *Sunday People -Boston Sunday Herald*; Oct. 27, 1991
16 Sue Ellen Thompson & Barbara W. Carlson; *Holidays, Festivals, and Celebrations of the World Dictionary* -1994; p.132
17 *Family New In Focus*; A division of James Dobson's *Focus On The Family*; Aired 10/14/94
18 *The Baptist Bulletin magazine* -Oct. 1989
19 *Observations* newsletter - November 1987, quoting from *What In The World*
20 Craig S. Hawkins; *Christian Research Journal* - Winter/Spring 1990; *The Modern World of Witchcraft*
21 Texe Marrs; *The Awful Truth About HALLOWEEN*; p.5
22 Owen S. Rachleff; *The Occult Conceit-A New Look at Astrology, Witchcraft and Sorcery*; pp.189-190
23 Catholic Encyclopecia - *CD Rom edition; Halloween*

24 *Christianity Today*; October 22, 1982; p.32
25 *The Oxford English Dictionary* -Second Edition, 1989; Vol. II p.386
26 Irene A. Park; *Seven High Pagan Masses and Halloween*; p. 1
21 James Napier; *Holiday Legends*; Halloween
28 *The World Book Encyclopedia*, 1977 edition, volume 9; Jack-0-Lantern
29 Owen S. Rachleff; *The Occult Conceit-A New Look at Astrology, Witchcraft and Sorcery*; p.190
30 John Ankerberg & John Weldon; *The Facts On Halloween*; Harvest House Publishers © 1996; pp.8-9
31 George William Douglas; *The American Book of Days*© 1970; pp.569
32 Hatch; *The American Book of Days* -3rd edition
33 Sue Hewitt; *The Sun*; Thursday, August 25, 1988; p.21
34 *Atlanta Journal & Constitution*; October 16, 1977 Associated Press quote
35 *Milwaukee Sentinel*; October 13, 1990; page 5, part 3
36 Peter Haining; *An Illustrated History of Witchcraft*
37 *The Encyclopedia Britannica* -11th Edition; Volume 28; page 755
38 Doreen Valiente; *An ABC of Witchcraft*; Phonenix Publishers 1988; p.343
39 Francis X. King
40 Sybil Leek; *Diary of A Witch*; Prentice-Hall, 1968; pp 17-19
41 William Schnoebelen; *Wicca - Satan's Little White Lie*; p.41
42 *Time Magazine*; May 6, 1991; p. 73
43 *Milwaukee Magazine*; October 1992
44 Steward Farrar; *What Witches Do*; Coward Mccann & Geoghean 1971
45 *Man, Myth & Magic* - Volume 14; Richard Cavendish Editor; Article on Modern Witchcraft
46 Ellen Evert Hopman and Lawrence Bond; *The People of The Earth*; Destiny Books (c) 1969; p. 139
47 Ibid.; p. 140
48 Ibid.; p.141
49 Ibid.; p. 143-144
50 *Circle Network News - Spring 1990*; p.6

PART 2

51 *The Encyclopedia of Witches And Witchcraft* by Rosemary Ellen Guiley; Facts on File 1989; p.63
52 *Satanism and the History of Wicca* by Diane Vera; Originally written January 1992
53 Charles G. Leland; *Aradia: Gospel of the Witches*
54 *Mastering Witchcraft* by Paul Huson; G.P. Putnam's Sons 1970, quote from book jacket
55 Ibid.; p.186
56 *A Witches Bible Compleat* by Janet and Stewart Farrar; Magical Childe Publishing; Volume2 p.21
57 *Devil Worship: The Rise of Satan*; Jeremiah Films
58 *Sybil Leek's Book of Curses* by Sybil Leek; Prentice-Hall 1975
59 Paul Huson; *Mastering Witchcraft*; book jacket review
60 *Cults That Kill* by Larry Kahaner; Warner Books; p. 99
61 *Witches* by Erica Jong; p.86
62 Ibid.; p.86
63 *At the Heart of Darkness* by John Parker; Citadel Press; p. 45
64 Ibid.
65 *Circle Network News* - Winter 95/96, Issue 58; p.24
66 Jack M. Roper, R.N.; *Paraphernalis Primer: Occult Bric A Brack*; p.3
67 *The Encyclopedia Britannica, Micropaedia*; volume 7, p. 469
68 Rosemary Ellen Guiley; *The Encyclopedia of Witches and Witchcraft*© 1989; Facts On File; p.240
69 Ibid.; pp.111-112
70 *Man, Myth & Magic* - Volume 14; Richard Cavendish Editor; vol.21, p.2889
71 Doreen Valiente; *An ABC of Witchcraft*; Phoenix Publishers 1988; p.128
72 Craig S. Hawkins; *Witchcraft*© 1996; Baker Books; p.33
73 Ibid.; p.33
74 Starhawk; *Spiral Dance*; p.29
75 Craig S. Hawkins; *Witchcraft*© 1996; Baker Books; p.36
76 Ibid.; p.38
77 Scott Cunningham; *Witchcraft Today*; p. 72
78 David Brown; Th.M.; *Chuck Colson Advances the New Age Religious Agenda*; p.4
79 Doreen Valiente; *An ABC of Witchcraft Past & Present*© 1973; p.333

80 Ibid.
81 Ibid.
82 W. B. Crow; *Witchcraft, Magic & Occultism*; Wilshire Book Company; p.250
83 *Mysteries of Mind, Space & Time*; H.S. Stuttman, Inc.; Vol. 26, p. 3124
84 Radu Florescu and Raymond T. NcNally; *Dracula, A Biography of Vlad the Impaler*
85 *Racine Journal Times*; August 9, 1998; p.5c
86 Ann Landers; *Milwaukee Journal; Parents must tackle violence*; January 6, 1988; p.8
87 David L. Brown; *File #13 Report - The Jeffery Dahmer-Occult Connection*; pp.3-4
88 George Will; *Studies show that television violence begets more violence*; Milwaukee Sentinel Thursday, April 8, 1993; p. 10a
89 *The Journal Times-Racine Wisconsin*; Wednesday, November 7, 1990; p.8a
90 *Milwaukee Journal*; Sunday, January 15, 1989; p. section 1B
91 *Milwaukee Journal Sentinel - Teen Describes 2 days of torture*; Tuesday, September 17, 1996
92 Chris Wood; *Maclean's Magazine*; March 30, 1987; p.54
93 Ibid.
94 *The Commercial Appeal* - West Memphis Newspaper; September 3, 1994

ENDNOTES—PART 2

1 Thomas Anderson; *Where Angels Walk*
2 Noah Webster; *The 1828 American Dictionary of The English Language;*
3 *Webster's New World Dictionary*; © 1968; The World Publishing Company
4 *Green Egg - Autumn 1995*; p.53
5 David L. Brown; *Cartoons: Primer of Paganism & The Occult;* p.4
6 Morning Glory Zell; *Green Egg/Autumn 1995*; p.53
7 Albert J. Dager; *Media Spotlight*; p.3
8 DIFFERENT WORLDS; *Issue 15; Favorites Of The Gods* by

PART 2

David F. Nalle; p.24-25
9 Ward & Kuntz; *Deities & Demigods* - TSR Games; p.103
10 Ibid. all the above deities mentioned
11 *Larousse Encyclopedia of Mythology*; Prometheus Press; 1960; p.444
12 *The Sunday Mail*; May 19, 1995; Australian Newspaper
13 Aimee Miller; *Washington Post - Under the Spell of 'Magic'*; 7-27-94
14 Georgia Pabst; *Milwaukee Journal Sentinel - Success of Fantasy Si-Fi Card Game Is Magical;* August 6, 1995
15 *Magic: The Gathering* - Deckmaster's Instruction Book
16 Aimee Miller; *Washington Post - Under the Spell of 'Magic'*; 7-27-94
17 Ibid.
18 George H. Baxter & Larry W. Smith, Ph.D.; *Mastering Magic Cards*; p.30
19 Ibid. p.30
20 Aimee Miller; *Washington Post - Under the Spell of 'Magic'*; 7-27-94;
21 Dr. Grace Kellerman, M.D.; *You and Your Child's Problems*

ABOUT THE AUTHOR

David L. Brown was born in Michigan. He came to know

Christ as his Savior as the result of a Sunday school teacher throwing away the liberal curriculum, teaching through the book of Romans, and sharing the Gospel. He has been married to Linda for 49 years. She was a young lady from his home church.

David attended a Michigan University then transferred to a Christian University and Seminary where he completed a Bachelor's Degree in Social Science and Theology. He holds a Master's Degree in Theology, and Ph.D. in History, specializing in the history of the English Bible.

Since December 1979, he has been the Pastor of the First Baptist Church of Oak Creek, Wisconsin (an independent, fundamental, Baptist Church using the King James Bible and conservative music). Previous to that, he pastored an independent Baptist Church in Michigan for five years, was an assistant pastor for 4 years, and served with his wife as short-term missionaries in Haiti.

Dr. Brown is the president of the **King James Bible Research Council**: (www.kjbresearchcouncil.com), an organization dedicated to promoting the King James Bible and its underlying texts and other traditional text translations around the world in a solid and sensible way.

He is also the president of **Logos Communication Consortium, Inc**. (www.logosresourcepages.org), a research organization that produces a large variety of materials warning Christians of present dangers in our culture. He is also the vice president of the **Midwest Independent Baptist Pastor's Fellowship**, a fellowship of independent Baptist pastors, missionaries, and evangelists from fourteen upper Midwest states.

Dr. Brown is the Curator of the **Christian Heritage Bible Collection** and regularly takes his rare Bible, manuscript and artifact collection to fundamental Baptist Churches teaching and preaching on the history of our English Bible, showing how God has preserved His Word(s), and why we should use the King James Bible.

He also serves as a consultant for individuals, museums, colleges, universities, and seminaries that desire to acquire or have collections of biblical manuscripts and Bibles. He is an antiquarian book dealer with contacts around the world.

Some of his other publications include:
1. *The Indestructible Book,* a 500 page, hardback with a cover
2. *The Indestructible Book, a 500 page, perfect bound book*
3. *God's Blueprint For Marriage & Family*, a perfect bound book, 108 pages
4. *The Defined Geneva Bible, New Testament, With Modern Spelling,* Editor, hardback, 344 pages
5. *The Geneva Bible, Old Testament, With Modern Spelling,* Editor, hardback, 970 pages.
(see the next page for contact information)

PART 2

He can be contacted at:

Dr. David L. Brown
8044 S. Verdev Dr.
Oak Creek, WI. 53154
Phone: 414-768-9754
Email: PastorDavidLBrown@gmail.com

www.ingramcontent.com/pod-product-compliance
Lightning Source LLC
Chambersburg PA
CBHW071713090426
42738CB00009B/1757